U.S. ARMY MOBILIZATION AND LOGISTICS IN THE KOREAN WAR A RESEARCH APPROACH

by

Terrence J. Gough

CENTER OF MILITARY HISTORY
UNITED STATES ARMY
WASHINGTON, D.C., 2011

Library of Congress Cataloging in Publication Data

Gough, Terrence J.
U.S. Army mobilization and logistics in the Korean War.

Bibliography: p.
Includes index.
1. United States. Army—Mobilization—History—
Korean War, 1950-1953. 2. Korean War, 1950-1953—
Logistics. 3. Korean War, 1950-1953—United States.
I. Center of Military History. II. Title.
UA913.G68 1987 355.2'8'0973 87-1781

First Printed, 1987—CMH Pub 70-19

For sale by the Superintendent of Documents, U.S. Government Printing Office
Washington, D.C. 20402

Foreword

In view of their crucial importance to military success, mobilization and logistics deserve thorough attention from historians. Although the Army's ability to mobilize has improved in recent years, much remains to be done, and the Korean War experience can provide valuable insights. Planners involved in the attempt to perfect current automated manpower mobilization systems need to prepare for possible strains and even collapse of those systems. In an emergency, we may have to rely on manual methods such as those that saw us through the Korean War.

Industrial preparedness also has received increased emphasis and support in the last decade. But in this area, as well, there is much to be learned from the Korean War's partial mobilization.

Finally, we can study with profit the problems encountered in supplying the large forces that we fielded in Korea. Planners who deal with theater logistics could benefit from detailed analysis, solidly grounded in original sources, of those problems and the solutions devised for them during the war.

This monograph should provide impetus to examine Korean War mobilization and logistics. Through a discussion of the available literature, the author presents an overview of the most pertinent issues addressed thus far. He then suggests how future investigators might elaborate on particular points, and offers topics that warrant further research.

Washington, D.C.   WILLIAM A. STOFFT
5 January 1987   Brigadier General, USA
                                          Chief of Military History

The Author

Terrence J. Gough received an A.B. degree in history and an M.A. degree in American history from the University of Miami in 1966 and 1974, respectively. Currently he is a candidate at the University of Virginia for a Ph.D. degree in American history, with a concentration in the period since the Civil War. After Army service as an enlisted man in the Military Police Corps from 1967 to 1969, which included a tour of duty in the Republic of Vietnam, he taught American history in the public schools of Dade County, Florida, for several years. Later a fellow at the Office of Air Force History and a historian with the federal Food and Drug Administration, he joined the Center of Military History in 1979. He has specialized at the center in the history of mobilization, logistics, and administration.

Preface

This study is intended to serve both as a general introduction to U.S. Army mobilization and logistics during the Korean War and as the foundation for further treatment of these subjects. As treated here, "mobilization" involves the assemblage and organization of manpower and materiel to support national objectives in an emergency. "Manpower mobilization" includes activation of reserve components; assemblage and organizing of personnel, supplies, and equipment; and major personnel policies that affect the composition of units in the field and in training. "Industrial mobilization" represents the process of transforming industry from its peacetime activity to the industrial program necessary to support national military objectives. "Logistics" involves planning and carrying out the movement and maintenance of forces.

Chapter 1 of the present effort consists of a chronological summary of major events. Like the other parts of the study, the chronology does not attempt to cover the Korean War in all its aspects. Readers interested in a general study of the war should consult David Rees' *Korea: The Limited War* (New York: St. Martin's Press, 1964) and Joseph C. Goulden's *Korea: The Untold Story of the War* (New York: Times Books, 1982), both of which contain extensive bibliographies.

Chapter 2 takes a bibliographical approach, laying out the pertinent issues as covered in both the available published literature and unpublished monographic sources (as of mid-1985). There is also a discussion of relevant archival material that seeks to indicate the value to the researcher of the various collections of documents and the problems that can be anticipated in their use. Chapter 3 attempts to crystallize the most salient issues raised or suggested in the second chapter and to propose others that warrant the historian's — and the soldier's — consideration. If this study stimulates investigation of at least some of these topics, it will have achieved its primary aim.

Many current and former colleagues at the Center of Military History gave generously of their time and expertise in the preparation of this study. Morris J. MacGregor, Jr., as chief of the General History Branch, provided patient counsel. Robert K. Wright, Jr.'s phenomenal knowledge of the entire spectrum of American military history and his perspective as a National Guard officer were particularly valuable. The Organizational History Branch, in the persons of Wayne M. Dzwonchyk, Stephen E. Everett, Rebecca R. Robbins, and John B. Wilson, expedited the study more than a few times with information on various units. Larry A. Ballard, Geraldine K. Judkins, and Hannah M. Zeidlik were unfailingly prompt and efficient in providing materials from the Historical Resources Branch. In the library, Carol Anderson and Mary J. Sawyer cheerfully and expertly filled numerous requests. Billy C. Mossman, drawing on his personal knowledge of events and many years of study, continued in retirement to be a gracious and dependable source of information on the Korean War. Two decades ago, Walter G. Hermes and his colleagues in the Current History Branch produced a "Chronological Listing of Important Decisions and Events Relating to the Mobilization and Force Development of the Army during the Korean War," which serves as the base upon which the chronology in the present study is built. Although he did not make a direct contribution, my retired colleague, James E. Hewes, Jr., provided a fine example of scholarly tenacity and dedication. My editor, Diane Sedore Arms, brought to the project not only fine editing skills but also the ability to apply them with equanimity and understanding; and she probably was right in excising those semicolons. Marshall T. Williams of the Production Staff proficiently prepared the graphics. Gina D. Wilson's word processing of the manuscript met her usual high standard, and Terrence L. Offer ably made the final revisions.

My debt to the staff of the National Archives and Records Administration is considerable. At the Military Field Branch, located at the Washington National Records Center in Suitland, Maryland, Richard L. Boylan, George C. Chalou, Ben Cooper, Jr., Wilmah M. Getchell, Jr., Morris Izlar, Frederick W. Pernell, and Victoria S. Washington combined to make my visits there pleasant and my research in official records possible. The same is true of Edwin R. Coffee, Terese E. Hammett, LeRoy Jackson, Wilbert B. Mahoney, and Edward J. Reese of the Military Reference Branch at the main National Archives building in Washington, D.C. William H. Cunliffe, chief of the Special Archives Division, shared once again his incomparable knowledge of military records.

Any errors of fact or interpretation are my responsibility alone.

Washington, D.C.   TERRENCE J. GOUGH
5 January 1987

Contents

vii

Illustrations

The following illustrations appear between pages 49 and 54:

Advance Detachment of the 71st Signal Service Battalion, Pusan Base
    Command
Draftees Wait for Their Physical Examinations
Inductees Are Sworn Into the Army
One Millionth Man Through the Port of Pusan
Trainees Listening to a Lecture
Incoming Inductees Pass Troops Bound for Korea
Trainees Receive Instructions on the Use of the Recoilless Rifle
Two Soldiers Wait Happily Outside the Rotation Office
Veterans of the Fighting in Korea, Homebound
Cross-section of the Troop Compartment Aboard a Troopship
Members of the 23d Infantry, 2d Infantry Division, After Debarking
    at Pusan
Troops of the 7th Infantry Division Land at Inchon Harbor

The following illustrations appear between page 83 and 90:

A Worker Welds an M-46 Tank Turret
Motor Equipment Waiting for Shipment to Korea
Ordnance Troops Repair Precision Instruments
Stockpiles of Military Supplies Along the Docks in the Port of Pusan
A Soldier Sorts Dirty Uniform Pants and Jackets
View of the Harbor and City of Pusan
LSTs and LCMs Stranded by the Low Tide in the Yellow Beach Area
    of Inchon
Large Piles of Supplies on the Docks at Inchon
Cargo Is Loaded From the SS *Carleton Victory* to a DUKW in Inchon
    Harbor
The U.S. X Corps Class I Dump at a Supply Point
Drums of Mobile Gas at a Reserve Point
A Steam Locomotive Is Hoisted From Ship to Dock at Pusan
South Korean Laborers and U.S. Soldiers Carry Ammunition and
    Food to Frontline Troops
The 187th Regimental Combat Team Receives Supplies From the Air
Troops Aboard an LST Prepare To Embark on an Evacuation Ship
    Waiting in Inchon Bay

All illustrations are from the files of the U.S. Army Center of Military
History except that at the top of page 83, which appears courtesy of
UPI/Bettman News Photos.

U.S. ARMY MOBILIZATION AND LOGISTICS IN THE KOREAN WAR
A RESEARCH APPROACH

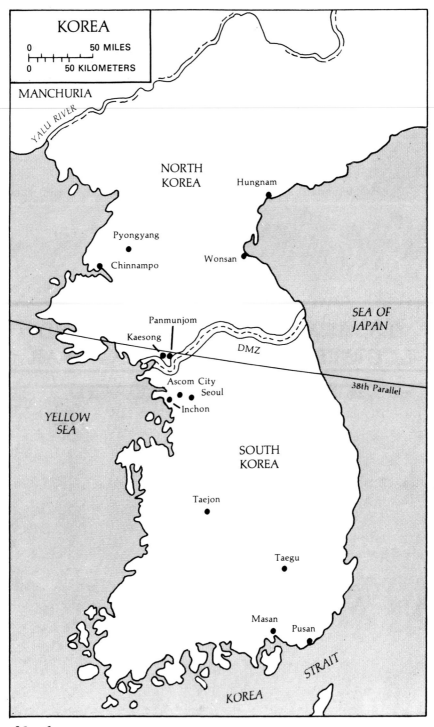

KOREA

0   50 MILES

0   50 KILOMETERS

MANCHURIA

YALU RIVER

NORTH KOREA

Hungnam

Pyongyang

Chinnampo

Wonsan

Panmunjom

Kaesong

DMZ

SEA OF JAPAN

Ascom City

Seoul

Inchon

38th Parallel

YELLOW SEA

SOUTH KOREA

Taejon

Taegu

Masan

Pusan

STRAIT

KOREA

MAP 1

CHAPTER 1
Chronology

1950

25 June: The Army of the People's Democratic Republic of Korea (North Korea) crossed the 38th Parallel and invaded the Republic of Korea.

27 June: The Senate Armed Services Committee initiated action on a call-up of reserve components.

30 June: Congress authorized the calling up of National Guard and Organized Reserve Corps units and individuals and set the term of service at twenty-one months.

30 June: President Harry S. Truman signed Public Law 599, which extended selective service until 9 July 1951.

30 June: General of the Army Douglas MacArthur, Commander in Chief, Far East Command, received authority from the president and the Department of the Army to employ U.S. ground combat forces in Korea. The actual strength of combat troops of the Eighth Army was 48.8 percent of normal authorization, and of service troops, 25.9 percent.

July: The Army stepped up recruitment and extended all existing terms of enlistment by twelve months; 20,000 enlistments were secured during the month. The first call for selectees was issued, with the induction date set for September.

1 July: Despite the outbreak of the Korean War, the transfer of the Army's ocean shipping to the Military Sea Transportation Service was completed smoothly.

4 July: By this time, the Pusan Base Command had been organized to support activities at that South Korean port. On this date, General Headquarters, Far East Command, established the Pusan Base Command as a subordinate command of the U.S. Army Forces in Korea to furnish logistical support for combat service forces ordered to Korea under the United Nations flag.

6 July: As part of an expansion of all armed forces, the Joint Chiefs of Staff and Secretary of Defense Louis A. Johnson recommended, and the president approved, the raising of authorized Army strength from 630,000 to 680,000.

7 July: In response to General MacArthur's urgent requests of 2–5 July for reinforcements in the Far East, the Joint Chiefs of Staff recommended to the secretary of defense that Army General Reserve units be sent to Korea.

8 July: The secretary of defense and the president approved the recommendation of the Joint Chiefs of Staff that Army General Reserve units be sent to Korea.

9 July: General MacArthur asked for an army of at least four divisions, with essential combat support and logistical services, in addition to the four divisions he already had.

10 July: Army Chief of Staff, General J. Lawton Collins, on a visit to Japan, informed MacArthur that he probably would have to fight with the 4 divisions on hand, which would be brought to full strength, plus 1 Army division, 1 regimental combat team, and 1 Marine division.

13 July: The Joint Chiefs of Staff recommended a second increase in the authorized strength of the Army to 740,500 men.

13 July: The Pusan Logistical Command, organized on the basis of a table of organization and equipment, replaced the Pusan Base Command.

14 July: The secretary of defense and the president approved the Joint Chiefs' request of 13 July.

14 July: The Joint Chiefs requested the secretary of defense to seek the approval of the president to call up National Guard units.

16 July: All ground forces of the Republic of Korea came under the command of the Eighth Army.

17 July: The first elements of the 2d Infantry Division sailed for Japan, where the division was to be staged for transport to Korea.

18 July: As the North Koreans neared Taejon, the Joint Chiefs of Staff requested a third increase in the Army's authorized strength, which would raise the total to 834,000.

19 July: Secretary of Defense Johnson and President Truman approved the Joint Chiefs' request of 18 July.

19 July: The president gave the secretary of defense authority to call up the National Guard and the Organized Reserve Corps.

21 July: The Department of the Army informed General MacArthur that his request for another army of four divisions could not be considered until defense officials had determined to what level the General Reserve would be rebuilt and the relative importance of Korea to other commitments worldwide.

1950

22 July: The Army requested reserve officers to volunteer for active duty.

25 July: The Far East Command submitted to the Office of the Assistant Chief of Staff, G–4, its requests for winter clothing and equipment.

27 July: The president signed Public Law 624, which extended enlistments in the armed forces for a period not to exceed twelve months. The Army increased its call of 10 July from 20,000 to 50,000, the inductees to be delivered not later than 30 September 1950, and set its October call at 50,000.

27 July: The Army announced the suspension of all disposals of serviceable and economically repairable surplus equipment.

31 July: The chief of staff proposed to the Joint Chiefs that four National Guard divisions and two National Guard regimental combat teams be called to active duty. He pointed out that the call-up would require lifting the Army's authorized ceiling to 1,081,000 spaces. The call-up would take place in September, with the divisions to be brought to full strength by November and to be prepared for combat by the summer of 1951. The Joint Chiefs approved.

31 July: After a change in plans, elements of the 2d Infantry Division, originally scheduled to stage in Japan, arrived in Korea directly from the United States.

1 August: Shipments of winter clothing and equipment to the Far East Command began.

3 August: Since the call for volunteers from the Organized Reserve Corps had failed to produce an adequate response, the Army resorted to an involuntary recall of enlisted men. The Army ordered 30,000 to report in September, with the bulk of the levies on the Volunteer and Inactive Reserve. Units in a paid drill status were maintained intact in the event of an emergency arising elsewhere.

3 August: Between 22 July and 3 August, 134 National Guard units received orders to report for active duty.

3 August: Congress, at the president's request, removed the existing limitations of the size of the Army.

10 August: With the Eighth Army hemmed in behind the Pusan Perimeter in Korea, the secretary of defense and the president approved the calling of four National Guard infantry divisions (the 28th, 40th, 43d, and 45th) and two regimental combat teams (the 196th and 278th) into federal service.

1950

10 August: The president approved the increase of the Army to an authorized strength of 1,081,000.

10 August: The Army was forced to initiate an involuntary recall program for reserve officers because of the poor response to the earlier call for volunteers; 7,862 reserve captains and lieutenants were ordered to report for duty in September and October.

12 August: The Headquarters and Headquarters Company, Pusan Quartermaster Base Depot, was organized to operate the base depot at Pusan.

20 August: The last elements of the 2d Infantry Division arrived in Korea.

23 August: Moving toward its expansion goal, the Army, in a second levy, recalled 77,000 members of the Organized Reserve Corps involuntarily.

25 August: Rear Headquarters of the Eighth Army in Yokohama, Japan, became the Japan Logistical Command. This headquarters, which had been fulfilling the duties pertaining both to logistical support for the Army in Korea and area administration in Japan, thus became, in effect, a theater communications zone organization. The G–4, Headquarters, Japan Logistical Command, was responsible for ensuring the provision of the supplies and equipment necessary to support the forces engaged in the Korean operations.

26 August: The first of two ships carrying the 65th Infantry (which later became the 3d Infantry Division's third regiment in place of the 30th Infantry), left Puerto Rico for Korea.

27 August: The second of two ships carrying the 65th Infantry left Puerto Rico.

30 August: The first of five ships carrying units of the 3d Infantry Division left San Francisco for Korea.

1 September: At the request of the Army, the Joint Chiefs of Staff submitted force requirements to Secretary of Defense Johnson. The Joint Chiefs recommended that seventeen Army divisions be approved for fiscal year 1951 and eighteen divisions for the succeeding three years.

1 September: The 40th and 45th Infantry Divisions, National Guard units, entered federal service, giving the Army a total of twelve combat divisions.

5 September: The National Guard's 28th and 43d Infantry Divisions entered federal service as the thirteenth and fourteenth Army

1950

combat divisions.

8 September: President Truman signed the Defense Production Act, which gave him power to allocate materials, grant production loans, establish priorities, control consumer credit, and impose wage and price controls.

9 September: President Truman announced that the chairman of the National Security Resources Board would coordinate administration of the powers given the president by the Defense Production Act. (The National Security Act of 1947 had created the National Security Resources Board to advise the president on the coordination of military, industrial, and civilian mobilization.) Distributing specific control duties among several agencies, Truman assigned responsibility for materials and facilities to Secretary of Commerce Charles Sawyer.

11 September: The secretary of commerce established the National Production Authority to handle priorities, allocations, and inventory controls.

15 September: Carrying out General MacArthur's bold plan, units of the U.S. Army X Corps landed at Inchon.

16 September: The last of five ships carrying units of the 3d Infantry Division arrived in Korea.

19 September: The 3d Logistical Command was activated in Japan. Its purpose was to provide logistical support to the X Corps. (An advance party of the 3d Logistical Command had been organized in Japan on 28 August and had landed at Inchon on 18 September.)

19 September: Because of an increasing burden of responsibilities, the Pusan Logistical Command was discontinued, and the 2d Logistical Command, a larger organization, was established. The primary mission of the new command was to receive, store, and forward supplies for the Eighth Army, and it was also responsible for forwarding most of the Eighth Army's requisitions to the Japan Logistical Command.

22 September: The second of the two ships carrying the 65th Infantry arrived at Pusan.

22 September: Since 15 September, over 6,000 vehicles, 25,000 tons of equipment and supplies, and 53,000 persons had been unloaded at Inchon.

27 September: In response to the Joint Chiefs' request of 1 September, Secretary of Defense George C. Marshall authorized the Army to plan for seventeen Army divisions and an increase in strength to 1,263,000 by the end of fiscal year 1951. He also authorized the Army to plan for eighteen divisions and a strength of 1,353,000 for fiscal year 1952.

1 October: The first ship carrying the 65th Infantry having broken down, and the troops having transferred to another ship at Pearl Harbor, the latter vessel arrived in Pusan.

7 October: The 3d Logistical Command, though remaining at its location between Inchon and Seoul, was attached to the 2d Logistical Command.

8 October: The 2d Logistical Command, a subordinate command of the Eighth Army, with headquarters at Pusan, received an administrative order from the X Corps requiring the Eighth Army to support the X Corps logistically for operations on the east coast. Although the order was technically improper, the 2d Logistical Command complied with it in order to accomplish the mission.

31 October: After the success of the Inchon landing and the rout of the North Koreans, the Far East Command forces pressed on toward the Yalu River. General MacArthur had 6 Army divisions, 2 regimental combat teams, 1 Marine division, and a total of 214,000 U.S. personnel under his command in Korea and Japan.

2 November: Based on the favorable progress of the war in Korea, Deputy Secretary of Defense Robert A. Lovett asked the Joint Chiefs of Staff to examine their force requirements and reduce them because of the drains upon the nation's economy and manpower resources. He indicated that the total of Army divisions should not exceed sixteen.

18 November: The 4th Division, formerly a training division, was redesignated the 4th Infantry Division and became the fifteenth Army combat division.

22 November: The National Security Council, acting on the recommendations of the Joint Chiefs of Staff, approved the fiscal year 1951 military program submitted by the secretary of defense. For the Army, the force structure was set at sixteen divisions with a strength of 1,263,000 at the end of June 1951 and eighteen divisions with a strength of 1,353,000 at the end of June 1954.

24 November: The U.S. Seventh Army was reactivated in Europe, and plans were made to build it up to two active Army and two National Guard divisions by the close of 1951.

1950

25 November: Forces of the People's Republic of China attacked, in strength, elements of the Eighth Army.

December: The change in the tactical situation resulted in the closing of the ports of Inchon, Wonsan, Hungnam, and Chinnampo.

2 December: The Eighth Army ordered the destruction of supplies that could not be evacuated before its withdrawal from North Korea.

3 December: General MacArthur requested immediate strong reinforcements lest his command suffer steady attrition possibly leading to final destruction.

5 December: In view of the intervention by the People's Republic of China, the Joint Chiefs of Staff recommended to the National Security Council that Army expansion be accelerated and that the total of eighteen divisions with a structural strength of 1,353,000, originally scheduled for attainment by June 1954, be reached by 30 June 1952.

5 December: Prompted by the wholesale loss of the equipment of two regimental combat teams during the enemy advance, Headquarters, Japan Logistical Command, asked General Headquarters, Far East Command, for authority to requisition enough equipment for two divisions and supporting troops. The Japan Logistical Command sought to preclude the possibility that a shortage of adequate replacement equipment to reconstitute combat units would jeopardize the Far East Command. Since the Department of the Army had already initiated shipment of equipment for one complete division, the Far East Command asked for equipment for a second division, but the Department of the Army disapproved this request.

6 December: Secretary of the Army Frank Pace, Jr., approved for planning purposes an Army staff plan for expanding the Army to twenty-one divisions with a strength of 1,530,000 men.

6 December: In answer to General MacArthur's request of 3 December, General Collins, the Army chief of staff, informed him that no replacements could be sent before the summer of 1951 and disapproved the sending of the only combat-ready division in the General Reserve—the 82d Airborne—on the grounds that this action would strip the General Reserve. The four National Guard divisions and the other three active Army divisions in the United States were in the process of being filled, equipped, and trained, and would not be available for shipment until mid-1951.

1950

9 December: Five of six ships carrying enough supplies for an entire division left San Francisco and Seattle for Korea. As part of a crash resupply program code named PINK, the supplies had been assembled, moved to the ports, and loaded within a week.

10 December: Having received an awaited air shipment from the East Coast, the sixth and last ship carrying PINK supplies left for Korea.

13 December: The chief of staff cautioned his Army commanders that the long lead time on equipment made gradual mobilization mandatory.

14 December: The National Security Council and the president approved the Joint Chiefs' recommendations of 5 December.

15 December: Operation SNAP, designed to receive and store in Japan supplies either evacuated from Korea or en route from the United States to Korea, began.

16 December: President Truman proclaimed a state of national emergency because of the seriousness of the Chinese intervention.

16 December: The president also signed Executive Order 10193, creating the Office of Defense Mobilization, headed by a director, to direct, control, and coordinate all mobilization activities of the executive branch.

16 December: Two National Guard infantry divisions, the 31st and the 47th, were ordered to report for active duty in January 1951.

18 December: General MacArthur requested that all four National Guard divisions recalled in September be moved to Japan.

18 December: Under Secretary of the Army Archibald S. Alexander signed a determination stating that, a national emergency having been proclaimed by the president, it was in the public's interest that purchases and contracts be negotiated without formal advertising during the period of the emergency.

22 December: The Joint Chiefs of Staff replied to General MacArthur's request of 18 December; they refused to commit additional divisions pending consideration at a higher level of the future course of U.S. actions in Korea.

22 December: The Army issued a third involuntary recall for 7,585 reserve officers, who would report in March 1951.

30 December: General MacArthur again requested that the four National Guard divisions be sent to Japan.

31 December: The actual strength of the Army totaled 1,073,498.

31 December: By this date, as a result of Operation SNAP, 18,957

1950

measurement tons of returned and backloaded cargo, and 107,047 measurement tons of diverted cargo, had been received in Japan.

1951

January: The 3d Logistical Command moved back to Pusan, where it remained a subordinate element of the 2d Logistical Command for the next two years.

3 January: By signing Executive Order 10200, President Truman established a Defense Production Administration to exercise general direction of the defense production program. The order delegated to the administrator of defense production the functions conferred on the president by the Defense Production Act relating to priorities and allocations. The president on 9 September 1950 had delegated these functions to the secretary of commerce.

9 January: The Joint Chiefs informed General MacArthur that if the Eighth Army could stabilize the situation in Korea and hold a line, two partly trained National Guard divisions could be sent to defend Japan but that if Korea had to be evacuated, the evacuated forces could defend Japan.

12 January: The president issued Executive Order 10202, which authorized selective service boards to allow men from eighteen through twenty-five years of age to volunteer for induction. These men could then be discharged after the 21-month draft period instead of having to serve the normal three years required of men who enlisted.

14 January: Lt. Gen. Matthew B. Ridgway, Commanding General, Eighth Army, criticized laxity on the part of unit commanders, which, he said, had resulted in the reckless abandonment of critical supplies and valuable equipment.

16 January: The 31st and 47th Infantry Divisions, National Guard units, entered federal service as the sixteenth and seventeenth combat divisions.

30 January: With the Eighth Army mounting a counteroffensive and driving north to the 38th Parallel once again, General Collins, the chief of staff, recommended that the National Guard's 40th and 45th Infantry Divisions be sent to the Far East Command in the spring. The Joint Chiefs approved.

1951

25 February: General MacArthur received notice that the two National Guard divisions would reach his command some time in April.

March: Under the supervision of the Eighth Army transportation officer, the Republic of Korea organized the Civil Transport Corps. Composed of Korean nationals, this corps provided human transportation of supplies for U.S. Army units.

7 March: The 1st Armored Division was reactivated and became the eighteenth Army division.

20 March: The Army requested an expansion of its authorized strength to 1,552,000 by the end of fiscal year 1951 to maintain the eighteen-division force, to sustain Korean operations, and to prepare for the replacement and rotation programs.

17 April: Secretary of Defense Marshall and President Truman approved the Army's request of 20 March for expansion of its authorized strength.

22 April: The Far East Command initiated its rotation program.

19 June: The president signed the Universal Military Training and Service Act, which extended selective service until 1 July 1955, lowered the draft age from nineteen to eighteen, increased the term of service from twenty-one to twenty-four months, and provided that men who had served in World War II be released after seventeen months of service. In addition, the act created a National Security Training Commission and charged it with submitting a broad outline for a universal military training program.

30 June: Since June 1950, the Army had expanded from 590,000 to over 1,530,000. The Army had recalled over 172,000 members of the Inactive and Volunteer Reserve and called up 34,000 from the National Guard, in addition to receiving 550,000 inductees through selective service.

July: The Japan Logistical Command began programmed shipments of supplies to Korea.

July: By this time, all supply depots in Korea, except an engineer depot at Inchon and a medical depot at Taegu, were located in the Pusan area. All Pusan depots were base-type depots, while the few outside the Pusan area were advance-type depots with very limited stocks.

10 July: Truce negotiations began in Kaesong.

14 July: At the request of the Eighth Army deputy commander, the Republic of Korea organized the Korean Service Corps. Recruited

1951

by the Republic of Korea Army, under whose discipline they served, the Korean nationals of this quasi-military corps provided general manual labor to U.S. Army units to which they were attached.

7 August: The chief of staff approved for planning purposes the Army long-range estimate for fiscal years 1952, 1953, and 1954 with a requirement for twenty-one divisions and the necessary supporting units.

15 August: The Joint Chiefs of Staff recommended that if combat operations in Korea lasted beyond 31 December 1951, the Army be increased to include 21 divisions, 18 regiments or regimental combat teams, and 117 antiaircraft artillery (AAA) battalions, and that the total authorized strength rise from 1,552,000 to 1,620,000.

18 August: The secretary of defense approved the Joint Chiefs' recommendations of 15 August in regard to the size of the Army.

23 August: The opposing side suspended truce negotiations temporarily.

29 August: The president approved the Joint Chiefs' recommendations of 15 August in regard to the size of the Army.

September: The National Guard's 37th and 44th Infantry Divisions were alerted to report for active duty in January and February 1952.

10 September: At the direction of the secretary of defense, the individual members of the Joint Chiefs of Staff proposed service strength estimates based on the assumption that the war would end by 31 December 1951. The chief of staff recommended to the Joint Chiefs that the Army contain 21 divisions, 18 regiments or regimental combat teams, and 117 AAA battalions in fiscal year 1953. Five of the divisions, two regimental combat teams, and forty-four AAA battalions would be maintained at reduced strength. The Army would have a strength of 1,596,000.

15 September: Secretary of Defense Marshall instructed the Joint Chiefs of Staff to submit an agreed-upon paper on strength levels, rather than individual recommendations.

17 September: The Joint Chiefs of Staff informed Marshall that they could not agree on force levels for fiscal year 1953.

5 October: Marshall approved the force levels recommended by the Army chief of staff on 10 September.

25 October: Truce negotiations resumed at Panmunjom.

28 October: In its first report to Congress, the National Security Train-

1951

ing Commission proposed six months of compulsory military training for all youths upon reaching the age of eighteen. Congressional action and presidential approval were necessary before any program could be put into effect.

October–November: In order to reach the strength totals approved in August, the Army requested selective service to provide 36,000 selectees in October and 29,000 in November.

November: In a merger designed to effect better recruitment and discipline, the Civil Transport Corps became part of the Korean Service Corps.

27 November: Negotiators at Panmunjom agreed on a geographic line of demarcation for a truce.

7 December: On the assumption that the war would be over by the end of December, the secretary of defense approved an Army strength of 1,596,000 as of 30 June 1952 instead of the 1,620,000 approved by the president on 29 August.

29 December: The Bureau of the Budget approved funds that would provide for an Army strength of only 1,552,000 men at the end of fiscal year 1952.

1952

January: By this time, 83 percent of the supplies moved from Japan to Korea were programmed shipments based on fairly accurate forecasts of firm requirements.

8 January: Secretary of the Army Pace asked Secretary Marshall for approval of a strength of 1,565,000 during fiscal year 1952, since a cutback to 1,552,000 would limit the expansion of Army divisions to twenty.

15 January: The National Guard's 37th Infantry Division entered federal service and became the nineteenth combat division.

18 January: The secretary of defense approved a strength level of 1,559,000 men for the Army at the end of fiscal year 1952.

February: By this time, 41 percent of all supplies shipped to Korea came directly from the United States.

15 February: The National Guard's 44th Infantry Division reported for active duty as the twentieth Army combat division.

16 February: The Joint Chiefs informed the secretary of defense that an increase in Army strength of 92,000 additional overhead spaces would be required because of the war's continuation into fiscal year

1952

1953, the release of large numbers of men who would have completed their terms of service, and the need to train recruits.

27 February: The secretary of defense disapproved an Army request for an end-of-fiscal-year strength of 1,599,900 and directed that the Army overstrength be eliminated by 30 June.

February–June: With the Army required to reduce to 1,552,000 men, selective service calls dropped to a level of 10,000 to 15,000 per month.

4 March: By a vote of 236 to 162, the House recommitted a universal military training bill to the Armed Services Committee for further study, thus killing the measure.

11 March: The Joint Chiefs of Staff recommended to the secretary of defense that he approve an Army strength figure of 1,644,000 for fiscal year 1953 because of envisioned worldwide commitments and an anticipated huge turnover of Army personnel.

21 March: The secretary of defense approved, for budgetary purposes, the Joint Chiefs' recommendation of an Army strength total of 1,644,000.

17 April: By signing Executive Order 10345, President Truman extended for nine months all enlistments due to expire in fiscal year 1952. The order affected 60,000 Army troops.

11 May: The secretary of defense gave the Army permission to close the fiscal year with a strength of 1,577,000.

14 June: General Collins, chief of staff, again requested that the Army be given 92,000 overhead spaces to handle training of new recruits and other worldwide missions. Although the Joint Chiefs and the secretary of defense approved, the increase failed to be adopted because of opposition by the Bureau of the Budget.

30 June: Despite the efforts of the Army to reduce its numbers, the total at the end of the fiscal year stood at 1,634,000, or 57,000 over the 1,577,000 level approved by the secretary of defense. By this time, approximately 500,000 men had been separated due to the expiration of terms of service of inductees and to legislative action requiring that reservists be released after seventeen to twenty-one months of service.

10 July: General Mark W. Clark, Commander in Chief, Far East Command, authorized the establishment of the Korean Communications Zone as a major command of the Far East Command.

30 July: Although the Army long-range estimate established a requirement for twenty-five divisions, the chief of staff told the Joint

1952

Chiefs of Staff that he would adhere to the 21-division level previously approved to avoid serious strains on the national economy. Actually, the Army had been unable to activate the twenty-first division because of budget and manpower restrictions.

1 August: The chief of staff informed Army commanders that they would lose half of the Army troops through rotation during fiscal year 1953. Some 750,000 men would have to be replaced by 650,000 recruits. The huge problem of training all the new men would affect the status and quality of the reserve forces in the United States, and each month would witness a lowering of the Army's proficiency and capability.

1 August: The 2d Logistical Command became, in effect, the Korean Base Section.

21 August: At the direction of General Clark, the Korean Communications Zone was established. From General Matthew B. Ridgway, Commanding General, Eighth Army, the communications zone took responsibility for logistical and territorial operations not immediately related to the conduct of combat operations in Korea and responsibility for political relations with the Republic of Korea. Physically, the Korean Communications Zone assumed authority for activities south of a boundary roughly approximating the 37th Parallel.

October: Despite the Army's efforts to secure approval of an increased strength figure because of the Korean War's continuation and the requirement to release and rotate large numbers of personnel, the administration refused to authorize a strength above the 1,552,000-man total. Secretary of Defense Robert A. Lovett, however, gave the secretary of the Army permission to present a package budget to support the 1,552,000-man figure if the war in Korea did not end during the fiscal year.

1 October: The Japan Logistical Command was discontinued. Its personnel, missions, and functions were absorbed by the reorganized U.S. Army Forces, Far East, which became the U.S. Army's major command in the Far East Command.

16 October: The 2d Logistical Command was officially transferred from the Eighth Army to the Korean Communications Zone (and was reduced to zero strength in November).

22 December: The Bureau of the Budget approved the Korean package for the size of the Army in fiscal year 1954. The Army would be permitted to have a beginning strength of 1,546,000 and

1952

an end-of-year strength of 1,543,000. If hostilities ended on 30 June 1953, the Army would be cut back to eliminate spaces provided in the package.

31 December: The Army fell below the 1,552,000 strength figure for the first time since July 1951 (and remained under that figure for the rest of the war).

1953

1 January: U.S. Army Forces, Far East, became the executive agency for the commander in chief, Far East Command, in administration and logistics and thus the principal administrative and logistical headquarters for the theater.

27 July: Representatives of the United Nations Command and the Korean People's Army and the Chinese People's Volunteers signed an armistice at Panmunjom that ended hostilities in the Korean War.

31 July: The actual strength of the Army was 1,526,921.

CHAPTER 2

The Issues: A Bibliographic Survey

Secondary Sources

General

More than thirty years after the event, there is no published comprehensive history of mobilization or logistics during the Korean War. Marvin A. Kreidberg and Merton G. Henry's *History of Military Mobilization in the United States Army, 1775–1945* (Washington, D.C.: Department of the Army, Government Printing Office, 1955; reprinted, with addition of index, 1984) — the reference "bible" for mobilization planners and historians — ends with the conclusion of World War II. In the standard comprehensive logistical history, *The Sinews of War: Army Logistics, 1775–1953* (Washington, D.C.: Office of the Chief of Military History, Government Printing Office, 1966), James A. Huston treats the Korean War in a single chapter based on his earlier, much longer, and unpublished manuscript history, "Korean Logistics," completed in June 1960. (Although Huston did this work under the auspices of the Office of the Chief of Military History, the only available copy is now in the records of that office in the Records of the Army Staff, Record Group 319, National Archives and Records Administration, Washington, D.C.) Huston published another condensation in "Korea and Logistics," *Military Review* 36 (February 1957), but the starting place for the in-depth researcher is the manuscript at the National Archives.

This unpublished logistical history is one of only a handful of detailed studies of Korean War mobilization and logistics. Of first importance for manpower mobilization and personnel policies are John Michael Kendall, "An Inflexible Response: United States Army Manpower Mobilization Policies, 1945–1957" (Ph.D. dissertation, Duke University, 1982); Historical Evaluation and Research Organization (HERO), "Mobilization in the Korean Conflict" (hereafter cited as HERO's "Mobilization") (Dunn Loring, Va., 1982); and Elva Stilwaugh, "Personnel Policies in the Korean Conflict" (Washington, D.C.: Office of the Chief of Military History, n.d.), microfilm copy in the U.S. Army Center of Military History. For logistics, the Huston manuscript should be consulted in conjunction with "Logistics in the Korean Operations," 4 vols. (Headquarters, U.S. Army Forces, Far East, and Eighth U.S. Army [Rear], 1955), microfilm copy in the Center of Military History.

The Center of Military History to date has published three volumes in its U.S. Army in the Korean War series: James F. Schnabel, *Policy and Direction: The First Year* (Washington, D.C.: Office of the Chief of Military History, Government Printing Office, 1972); Roy E. Appleman, *South to the Naktong, North to the Yalu* (Washington, D.C.: Office of the Chief of Military History, Government Printing Office, 1961); and Walter G. Hermes, *Truce Tent and Fighting Front* (Washington, D.C.: Office of the Chief of Military History, Government Printing Office, 1966). A fourth, Billy C. Mossman's "Ebb and Flow," now in manuscript form, is scheduled to be published in 1987. This volume will cover combat operations from November 1950, where Appleman leaves off, to July 1951, where Hermes begins. While useful for the strategic and tactical background of mobilization and logistics, these books do not approach the aforementioned unpublished studies in depth of treatment of mobilization and logistics. In the case of logistics, the center's plan for the series has long included a separate volume on the subject; thus, the authors of the other volumes purposely did not devote much space to it. The plan does not provide for a separate work on mobilization, so there is a modicum of attention rendered manpower mobilization in the Schnabel and Hermes books. Schnabel makes clear his approach to manpower issues when he states that he discusses "only the most significant measures" and refers the reader to Stilwaugh's monograph for "a comprehensive study."[1] Hermes' approach is similar.

None of these four official histories deals with industrial mobilization, an aspect very largely neglected by government and nongovernment historians alike. One exception is Harry B. Yoshpe's *A Case Study in Peacetime Mobilization Planning: The National Security Resources Board, 1947–1953* (Washington, D.C.: National Security Resources Board, 1953). Useful for details of the role of one of the several economic mobilization agencies of the war, this study lacks the perspective that a postwar view might have afforded. A comprehensive appraisal of the Korean War experience in industrial mobilization remains to be written. Roderick L. Vawter's *Industrial Mobilization: The Relevant History* (Washington, D.C.: National Defense University Press, 1983) includes a Korean War chapter that serves as a handy precis, but this slim book's title is unfortunate in view of the fact that the author relies solely on printed sources.

---

[1]Schnabel, *Policy and Direction*, p. 119, *n.* 13.

Prewar Plans and Policies

Kendall's "An Inflexible Response" is the premier source for prewar manpower mobilization planning. Using archival material extensively, he confirms the conclusion of HERO's "Mobilization" that initial post-World War II Army plans called for all-out mobilization but that limited funds and the slow pace of the organization of reserve forces made these plans unrealistic. Kendall explains President Truman's argument that low defense budgets helped keep a strong economy, which was a must for any future industrial mobilization. But he goes on to show that these budgets directly affected the Army's ability to complete its planned mobilization structure. The Army also had to cope with a National Guard that was virtually nonexistent at the end of World War II. With guardsmen released as individuals, rather than as units, all National Guard divisions were deactivated by 1946. What remained of the National Guard had to compete with an equally weak Organized Reserve Corps (ORC) for money, men, and equipment. Kendall is at his best in illuminating the political motivations of decisions involving the reserve components and the Army's quest for universal military training. As a solution to manpower problems, universal military training foundered on the shoals of political infeasibility.

In Kendall's account of military unreadiness for the Korean War, the Army does not go without criticism. Realizing by the end of 1946 that mobilization goals could not be met without the aid of universal military training, planners developed War Department Mobilization Plan I, which relied heavily on the reinduction of World War II veterans. The plan assumed a war similar to World War II and proposed a strategy virtually the same as the one that had proved successful in that conflict. Mobilization was to be slow, with large-scale overseas deployments scheduled to begin two years after M-day. "The staff planners," Kendall observes, "tried to follow the Army's historical precedent of being able to fight the next war by preparing for the last conflict" and developed no innovative solutions to mobilization problems.[2] Not only did they fail to understand the nation's needs in the nuclear age, Kendall believes, they also ignored many of the realities of the process of expansion for mobilization, such as the time required to prepare cadres and inactive camps for unit training and to integrate filler troops into regular units. Further, they were too confident that mobilization could begin during a warning period before an attack.

---

[2]Kendall, "Inflexible Response," p. 87.

When the Korean War broke, the Army was in transition from War Department Mobilization Plan I to Army Mobilization Plan II. Although the new plan showed some improvements over its predecessor, particularly in dropping the assumption of warning, Kendall scores it for continuing to envision only a big war against a first-rate power. He is critical, too, of its unreasonably optimistic estimates of the time required to mobilize, in comparison with the reality of the events of the second half of 1950.

Kendall provides a valuable account of the parlous state of the reserve components between 1945 and 1950 — an important element in the difficulties of mobilization that John K. Mahon's *History of the Militia and the National Guard* (New York: Macmillan, 1983) also treats. The National Guard lacked sufficient armories, Regular Army instructors, and money, and experienced problems in recruiting. Equipment also was inadequate, and the guard had no control over equipment in hand because it had no system of centralized property accounting. On the plus side, the political activities of the National Guard Association benefited the guard in the form of increased appropriations in a period during which other defense appropriations were declining. Yet even this advantage sometimes seemed only the silver lining in the cloud of political interference with military decisions.

Funding problems in the Organized Reserve Corps, which lacked the guard's political base, were more severe. Like the guard, the organized reserve was understrength and short of equipment and in-structors. In addition, it suffered from rank-heaviness and had poor unit cohesiveness due to the employment of composite units — that is, units composed of veterans who had not served in the same wartime units or branches. Since there was no money to provide pay for in-active training, the organized reserve started with a handicap in its attempts to form units. Incompletely organized into units, it presented the War Department (and later the Department of the Army) with a struggle to keep track of the reservists' location, civilian skills, and physical condition. In *Twice the Citizen: A History of the United States Army Reserve, 1908–1983* (Washington, D.C.: Office of the Chief, Army Reserve, 1984), Richard B. Crossland and James T. Currie amplify Kendall's treatment of these difficulties.

As if the various burdens borne by the Regular Army and the reserve components were not enough, Kendall finds that the several organizations "lacked a fundamental understanding of the traditions and needs of each other in the Army of the late 1940s." He concludes that "the manpower mobilization potential of the nation was largely wasted because of this lack of understanding."[3]

Interagency differences contributed also to a less than fully successful effort in industrial mobilization planning. Yoshpe's *A Case Study in Peacetime Mobilization Planning* and Steven L. Rearden's *History of the Office of the Secretary of Defense*, vol. 1, *The Formative Years, 1947–1950* (Washington, D.C.: Historical Office, Office of the Secretary of Defense, 1984) make this clear in their discussions of the evolution and functions of the Munitions Board and the National Security Resources Board (NSRB). The National Security Act of 1947 provided for both these entities, the National Security Resources Board being a new creation and the Munitions Board a continuation of an older Army and Navy Munitions Board. Theoretically confined to the military aspects of industrial mobilization, the Munitions Board used its advantage of an existing organization to control wider areas of planning responsibility. The National Security Resources Board, charged with advising the president on the coordination of military, industrial, and civilian mobilization, faced an uphill battle to establish an effective staff, smooth operating procedures, a clear-cut identity, and prestige. Squabbling between the two agencies over functions and other issues foiled attempts at settlement, and planning suffered. By the beginning of the Korean War, the NSRB's emergency role was still uncertain.

In *Industrial Mobilization*, Vawter praises the industrial mobilization plan developed by the Munitions Board in 1947 for its emphasis on predetermination and allocation of sources of supply and on elimination of competition among procurement agencies for the output of indvidual plants. He also applauds the Munitions Board for its efforts to stimulate planning programs within industry. The primitive state of historical scholarship on post-World War II industrial and economic mobilization plans and policies, however, precludes any substantial evaluation of these activities.

Vawter's description of the phases of mobilization envisioned in the 1947 plan makes clear the planners' belief that there would be sufficient time between the president's decision for mobilization and a declaration of war by Congress to implement plans, programs, and procedures in an orderly and effective manner. The National Security Resources Board took over and, by 1950, altered this plan, but the available literature does not reveal either the revised plan's contents

---

[3]Ibid., pp. 154–55.

or the relationship of the plan to the actual mobilization for the Korean War.

Planning aside, Vawter stresses the debilitating effects on the industrial base of rapid demobilization after World War II. To stimulate the civilian economy, the government sold most of the industrial plants whose construction had been federally financed during the war. A huge surplus of equipment and ammunition made industrial preparedness seem to many an item of low priority. Those plants not sold began to deteriorate because of inadequate appropriations for maintenance. Vawter cites an estimate that an expenditure of $50 million for plant maintenance from 1945 to 1950 would have saved $200 to $300 million in rehabilitation costs during the Korean War.

As for operational logistics planning—how to get supplies and equipment, once produced, from the United States to the troops in the theater—the failure of war planners to foresee the possibility of a North Korean invasion of South Korea meant that there was no war plan to form a basis for logistical planners. Presumably, then, there were no logistical plans for operations in Korea, and the literature reflects this presumption. However, in a letter to the editor of *Army*, July 1985, Col. Donald McB. Curtis (USA, Ret.) claims that the plans division of G-4, Army General Staff, in the fall of 1948 initiated a series of strategic logistic studies that included one for an invasion of South Korea across the 38th Parallel. According to Curtis, he, as a member of the division's strategic plans section, prepared a strategic concept that called for "a retreat to and defense of the Pusan perimeter, buildup and breakout, *and an amphibious landing at Inchon* to cut enemy supply lines." The purpose of these strategic logistics studies, Curtis states, was to "ascertain in advance what unusual logistic requirements could be expected in various potential theaters of operation."[4] Although he also states that other sections of the General Staff concurred in his strategic concept, he does not make clear whether special logistical support requirements were ever computed in conjunction with it. (His main concern is to challenge General MacArthur's parentage of the idea for the Inchon invasion.) A revision of the accepted wisdom that there were no logistical plans for the Korean War awaits a testing of Curtis' claim through thorough archival research.

---

[4]Curtis, *Army*, July 1985, p. 5 (emphasis in the original).

The Emergency

Troop strength and readiness were two large problems that faced the U.S. Army when the surprise invasion of South Korea demanded action in the summer of 1950. Assigned strength of the Regular Army on 26 June, worldwide, was 630,201, of whom 360,063 were in the continental United States. Of the remainder, 108,550 were in the Far East Command (nearly 10,000 below authorized strength) and 80,018 in Europe, with the rest scattered about the globe. The strength ceiling of the National Guard was 350,000, and the Organized Reserve Corps had a strength of 255,000. Approximately 185,000 students were enrolled in the Reserve Officers' Training Corps. (These figures are from Huston's "Korean Logistics.") Of this situation, Kendall states simply that "General MacArthur's Far East Command was in the worst condition that it had been in since the end of World War II" and notes that

it consisted of four divisions, the 24th, 25th, [and] 7th Infantry Divisions and the 1st Cavalry Division, in Japan and one Regimental Combat Team (RCT) in Okinawa. Unfortunately, all of these divisions had demobilized their medium tank battalions because they were too heavy for the Japanese bridges. Although each had an authorized wartime strength of nearly 19,000 men, in June of 1950 they actually had only two-thirds of this number. Manpower cuts had forced MacArthur to reduce his infantry regiments to two battalions instead of the authorized three. Similarly, his artillery battalions had been cut to two batteries instead of the usual three. This meant that the commanders would find it difficult if not impossible to maintain a tactical reserve in combat, nor could they rotate units out of the front line to rest them in the usual way.[5]

Stilwaugh's "Personnel Policies in the Korean Conflict" adds that the units largely consisted of young and inexperienced soldiers, armed with police-type weapons. By mid-July three of MacArthur's divisions were in Korea; as Stilwaugh and Kendall point out, the 7th Division, which remained in Japan, had to be skeletonized to make the other units deployable. The 29th Regimental Combat Team, reduced to two full battalions, went to Korea as a replacement unit for the divisions.

General MacArthur's efforts, as described by Stilwaugh, to fill out combat units included a sweep of every U.S. military nook in Japan to find general service personnel with combat experience or potential. Once located, they were replaced with members of the Women's Army Corps, Department of the Army civilians, or indigenous labor.

---

[5]Kendall, "Inflexible Response," pp. 164–65.

MacArthur then placed a levy on all organizations in Japan that were not under orders to deploy to Korea. The Army's Career Guidance Program, under which officers were placed in military occupational specialties, proved an impediment in shifting personnel. Many officers with the leadership ability and training experience so sorely needed in combat units could not be placed in command of troops, because their noncombat specialties had been mandated under the career program.

General MacArthur's personnel requirements forced immediate changes in the Army's worldwide rotation system. Effective 31 August 1950, the Army extended foreign service tours in all commands except the Far East for six months beyond the normal tour—the first of a series of such measures, as Stilwaugh notes. In the Far East Command, MacArthur received authorization to extend foreign service tours as the military situation required. The Army revoked the orders of personnel scheduled for overseas movement, except to the Far East Command.

Kendall's "An Inflexible Response" and James F. Schnabel and Robert J. Watson's *The History of the Joint Chiefs of Staff: The Joint Chiefs of Staff and National Policy*, vol. 3, *The Korean War*, Part 1 (Wilmington, Del.: Michael Glazier, 1979) lay out the dangerous manpower situation in which the United States now found itself. MacArthur quickly increased his estimate of the forces needed to handle the Korean emergency as conditions on the battlefield worsened. By the end of the first week in July, he had scrapped his call for two divisions and was asking for a field army of 4 divisions, 1 airborne regimental combat team, 1 armored group of 3 medium tank battalions, and numerous artillery and support units from the General Reserve in the United States. He also requested 30,000 additional men in order to bring the units in Japan to full strength. How the General Reserve, with six divisions, only one of which was ready for deployment, could meet these requirements was the question that faced the Joint Chiefs of Staff.

Meanwhile, Army logisticians had their own problems. In "Korean Logistics," Huston says that supplies on hand in the Far East Command at the beginning of the war were sufficient only to sustain troops in peacetime activities for sixty days. The theater history, "Logistics in the Korean Operations," indicates that levels in the various supply classes ranged from 45 to 180 days, with the majority falling into the 45- to 60-day range. Huston goes on to observe that supplies in the pipeline amounted to only a trickle. He also notes that while large quantities of equipment from deactivated units were available, most of this material was unserviceable, and repair operations could do little more than supply the current needs of the occupation forces. A significant portion of the repairable equipment had to be taken back from the Japanese Ministry of International Trade and Industry, to which the U.S. government had given large stocks of surplus property as a stimulus to the Japanese economy. In the scramble to equip divisions bound for Korea, the theater history relates, normal supply procedures and accountability went by the boards.

Along with the supply shortage, the command had to face a severe understrength in service troops. If combat elements of the Eighth Army were woefully undermanned at just under 50 percent strength, then service units were twice as bad off at 25.9 percent. The theater history makes clear that this situation was not wholly the result of peacetime levels of troop allocation; the Eighth Army had placed primary dependence for service support on local civilian employees.

Nor did the outlook for supplies and equipment, in Huston's view, seem good in the United States. He puts the level of depot stocks in the United States in late June 1950 at about ninety days for most supplies—and shipments for the Mutual Defense Assistance Program were depleting these. He explains that for purposes of planning, logisticians assumed that for each division in combat there should be equipment for an additional one-and-a-half division "slices" in reserve for each year of combat commitment. Plans therefore called for equipment for 103 division slices to be available on M-day. But the budget being prepared in 1950 allowed for equipment for only fifty-five division slices to be available by the end of 1952. Huston points out elsewhere in his discussion that this planning assumed an all-out mobilization—something that is obvious from the figures involved. Thus the shortage envisioned in the figures is more a measure of the planners' perception of difficulty at the beginning of a full-scale war than of the actual situation as it developed. Although Huston provides figures on the amount of various items of equipment available in the emergency, he does not make a detailed appraisal of the effect of this availability on readiness. He does make the point that Army reserve stocks were seriously unbalanced, so that even active units could not be fully supplied with modern equipment. Further, he notes that Army logistics planners considered the numbers of available installations for logistical support to be critically inadequate for mobilization—here again, a full mobilization. What Huston's discussion lacks is an explicit evaluative context. Is the basis for judgment of readiness the Army's ability to meet the immediate emergency of Korea, or is it preparedness for a larger, perhaps global struggle centered in Europe?

Huston makes clear that the Army did meet its critical supply and equipment needs early in the war by drawing on World War II stocks, which "saved the day."[6] The worst shortages naturally occurred in items of equipment, such as the 4.2-inch mortar and the recoilless rifle, that had been heavily emphasized in tables of organization and equipment (TOEs) since World War II. Stocks of items of supply, such as rations, mostly containerized and less susceptible to technological change, proved sufficient until production could begin.

The theater history emphasizes the importance during the emergency of shifting equipment from civilian component units and other sources, such as troops not scheduled for early movement and post and station stocks, to units scheduled for deployment to the Far East. Huston observes, saliently, that equipment in the possession of the National Guard was more readily usable than that in reserve stocks because the guard was responsible for maintaining its equipment in serviceable condition.

The General Reserve

On balance, the most crucial problem facing the Army in the emergency was manpower. To meet General MacArthur's quickly escalating demands for troops, the national command authorities could not wait for mobilization of reserve components or induction of draftees to begin. Congress in July passed legislation extending enlistments for a maximum of one year and lifting personnel ceilings, but these measures Kendall describes as stopgap. Initial reliance had to be on the General Reserve, "that portion of the United States Army, normally located in the continental United States, whose primary mission is to be trained, equipped, and maintained in a state of readiness for immediate use in an offensive or defensive role."[7]

To provide men rapidly for the Far East Command, the Army placed levies on individuals and units in zone of interior commands. As a result, the General Reserve gave up half of its combat units (infantry, tank, and artillery) and half of its support units to MacArthur. Stilwaugh cites an estimate by the Army G-3, in late July 1950, that at least a year would be required for the General Reserve to regain a state of readiness equal to that of June 1950. Kendall

---

[6]Huston, "Korean Logistics," ch. III, p. 46.
[7]SR 320-5-1, Dictionary of United States Army Terms, Aug 50.

refers to the "devastation of individual units in the general reserve," which he finds "appalling." "The mobilization actions," he declares, "had sacrificed the critical fighting quality of combat units, espirit [*sic*] and camaraderie, for expediency."[8] He cites as an important negative effect of these actions a severe reduction in the number of Regular Army men available to train reservists and inductees.

Stilwaugh explores the reasons behind this "woeful situation." "First, mobilization planning in effect prior to the Korean Conflict did not envision the commitment of Army forces overseas during the first year of mobilization. This thinking eliminated the requirement for producing combat loss replacements prior to the first year of war. Allied to this was the fact that budgetary limitations imposed by Congress held the General Reserve to a pitiable understrength and left it without the means of immediate augmentation for an emergency."[9]

Mobilizing Reserve Forces

In the first week of the emergency, it was clear that meeting the North Korean offensive would deplete the General Reserve. If aggression came from elsewhere, that reserve could not well serve as a foundation for reconstituting the mobilization base. Congress therefore acted quickly to give President Truman power to employ reserve forces and to obtain draftees through selective service. Congressional authorization was necessary since the president had not declared a national emergency (he did not take this step until after the November 1950 intervention by the People's Republic of China).

To provide sorely needed individual replacements, the Army had to look, as Kendall shows, to the Organized Reserve Corps. The organized reserve contained World War II veterans who could be trained quickly because the Army's equipment had changed little in the five years since the end of that war. HERO's "Mobilization" conveys well the difficulties that reliance on the organized reserve entailed. Insufficient funds and low recruiting rates had prevented organization of all organized reserve units at full strength, which would have required 146,000 officers and 956,000 men. The fiscal 1951 budget allowed for only 73,500 officers and 181,500 men in troop units, and even these much more modest levels had not been achieved by June 1950. Many combat and service support units stood at one-quarter, or less, of their enlisted strength when the war broke.

[8]Kendall, "Inflexible Response," p. 171.
[9]Stilwaugh, "Personnel Policies in the Korean Conflict," frame 506. (References to this study are from the microfilm copy in the Center of Military History.)

Awaiting the issuance of authority to begin involuntary call-ups, the Army in July sought both enlisted and officer volunteers from the Organized Reserve Corps for active duty of one year. This effort, which HERO's "Mobilization" describes as a conscious stopgap on the Army's part, involved special considerations in the case of the officers. In mid-1950 there were many reserve officers who had been serving on extended active duty since World War II and who had not been promoted since 1945; some of them held higher rank in the organized reserve than the rank in which they were serving. There were also many regular officers who were serving in grades reduced from those that they had held in World War II. These situations were juxtaposed to that of many reserve officers who had received terminal promotions at the end of the war. The HERO study points out that if the Army had permitted an influx of these senior reserve officers, they would have unfairly outranked those who had been on active duty in the postwar years. Therefore, the Army limited its call for officers to the grades of captain and lieutenant, thereby giving the active duty officers an opportunity to be promoted. Fortunately, this decision comported with the need for a greater number of officers in the junior than in the senior grades. According to the HERO study, only a few hundred field grade officers, in scarce and critical specialties, received individual recall notices during the Korean War.

By mid-July the Army received authority to recall reservists involuntarily, and Kendall and HERO make it evident that the power came none too soon. The voluntary call had produced pallid results, as the following figures, given by HERO, suggest: by the end of the war's first year, 43,000 officers and 125,000 enlisted men had to answer involuntary Army recalls.

Stilwaugh and HERO discuss some of the difficulties that involuntary recalls involved. The burden fell heavily on inactive reservists who had not expected to don uniforms again unless there was an all-out war. It seemed odd that those least prepared were the first to be called, while active, paid members of the organized reserve whose military skills were sharper remained at home. According to Stilwaugh, the Army's rationale was that the active reservists, because they were better prepared, had to be husbanded for any greater emergency that might arise. To judge from the public outcry that Stilwaugh and HERO both mention, those affected by the recall decisions took little solace in this explanation (if in fact the Army disclosed its reasoning—a point left unclear in both studies).

The Army, Stilwaugh reveals, suffered from a hazy knowledge of the status of its reservists. There had been no requirement since February 1947 that reservists undergo periodic physical examinations, so the number who would qualify physically for service was unknown in 1950. As it turned out, large numbers did not meet minimum physical standards. Many more reservists than anticipated had to be called in order to fill quotas, with the resultant administrative overhead and delays. Further delays stemmed from the handling of cases in which men's economic status had changed to the point that active duty would cause undue hardship. Stilwaugh describes personnel records on officer reservists as "inadequate" and on enlisted men as "virtually non-existent."[10]

HERO's "Mobilization" scores the Army's "unclear and inconsistent" policies concerning reservists reporting for service.[11] At first allowing twenty-one days between notification and reporting, the Army later reduced the period to fifteen days. Because of travel, paperwork delays, and processing time, some reservists had less than a week to put their affairs in order. Instead of making comprehensive announcements on deferment policies, the Department of the Army fed the public this information piece by piece, then neglected to publicize later changes sufficiently. The confusion engendered by these methods was only deepened by policy disparities among the various armed services, each of which initially regulated its own activities in this sphere. Department of Defense efforts to impose uniformity were largely successful by the end of 1950, but the HERO study notes that military necessity precluded complete standardization of policy.

Kendall weighs in with further criticism, zeroing in on the first involuntary recall. The Army staff assigned a quota to each of the six field armies. Although designed to ensure a fair distribution, this move also virtually guaranteed that there would be a variety of procedures. When some of those recalled requested exemptions for reasons of dependents, educational status, or occupation, the field armies often found that personnel records were too incomplete to make informed decisions. Consequent orders for the reservists to report to their post of assignment so that a proper determination could be made worked extra hardships. The need for men with special military skills, especially in the combat arms, dictated the recall of disproportionate numbers of veterans. Kendall notes also

---

[10]Ibid., frame 523.
[11]HERO, "Mobilization in the Korean Conflict," p. 24.

that the higher the level of skill required in civilian occupations, the greater was the percentage of reservists in that occupation. This situation presented the dilemma of depleting essential civilian occupations in order to get reservists into uniform. Not of the Army's making, this problem is a perennial for manpower specialists.

The National Guard, having conducted a nationwide recruiting drive late in 1949, was in better shape than the Organized Reserve Corps but was not without its own problems. On 30 June 1950 the guard's strength stood at 324,761, including 29,082 officers and 295,679 enlisted men, organized in 25 infantry divisions, 2 armored divisions, 20 regimental combat teams, and numerous support units of battalion size or smaller. Average strength for the infantry divisions was 61 percent, with individual divisions ranging from 46 to 82 percent. Plans called for six guard divisions to be maintained in a special readiness status. HERO's "Mobilization" cogently observes, however, that there was a legal requirement for the federal government to apportion funds for the guard in proportion to the number of enlisted men in the units of each state. With this stricture, the Army had to maintain all guard divisions at approximately equal levels of readiness, in effect thwarting the plans for selective readiness.

The political element evident in the distribution of funds was also present in the selection late in July 1950 of National Guard units for mobilization, and both HERO and Kendall treat the situation candidly. General Mark W. Clark, Chief of Army Field Forces, selected units for federalization on the bases of training, equipment, and readiness. Geographical distribution loomed large in the minds of those on the Army staff, however, and Clark's selections were bunched in the East. Only two of the four divisions mobilized, in addition to two regimental combat teams also picked by the staff, appeared on Clark's original list. Each of the final selections came from the geographical area of one of the six field armies. In partial defense of this decision, it is well to note Kendall's observation that movement of too many divisions from the East Coast would have worsened an existing transportation problem.

None of the guard units mobilized was up to strength. All of them sought a remedy in last-minute recruiting in the month between their alert and their scheduled federalization on 1 September. HERO and Kendall describe the mixed results. Alerted units reported gains of from 10 to 41 percent during the period, but the number of men recruited did not offset concurrent losses due to discharges and deferments. According to HERO, over half of the discharges resulted from discoveries that the men were under seventeen years old. Kendall notes that guardsmen remained under control of the states until they were federalized and that this permitted state adjutants general to release men who held critical civilian occupations or who had several dependents. An interesting problem that the HERO study explores is that of the guardsman enlisted at the last minute—often equipment was not available for him, he did not have the skills that the unit needed, and he tended to commit more disciplinary offenses.

Incomplete training of those already in guard units, combined with the need to train inductee fillers, meant that the National Guard could not be deployed for at least nine months after activation. In a measured judgment, Kendall appraises the guard as "clearly not the M-day force it had expected to be," although it constituted "a substantial part of the available general reserve and was at a generally better level of readiness" than all but one of the few remaining regular divisions.[12]

Once mobilization was under way, the Army encountered many hitches resulting largely from a general failure to rationalize and standardize policies among the various parts of the mobilization apparatus. HERO's "Mobilization" cites the difficulty of having to do many things in a short time with too few resources but faults Army planners for not fully foreseeing this situation. The HERO study also criticizes the planners for insufficiently anticipating the problems engendered by administrative pecularities in relations between the active Army and the reserve components. Not until after the mobilization had begun, Kendall states, did the Army notify National Guard units of changes in administrative procedures required to bring the guard into conformance with the Regular Army. HERO judges the execution of Army induction policies and procedures to be inefficient and confused. Separate induction regulations covering the Organized Reserve Corps and the National Guard were unnecessarily dissimilar. Policies in regard to delays and deferments were unclear and inadequately disseminated. Formats for orders varied from one army area to another. Because the Department of the Army sometimes did not issue movement directives promptly, units had trouble procuring the vehicles and packing equipment they required.

Military districts, to which the Army delegated responsibilities for administering individual and unit inductions, felt the effects of inadequate resources. HERO's "Mobilization" contains a good, suc-

---

[12]Kendall, "Inflexible Response,"pp. 177-78.

cinct discussion of shortcomings of district staffs, which included insufficient size and unfamiliarity with National Guard organization
and procedures. There was a particularly acute shortage of medical
personnel, both on district staffs and in the units being inducted.
HERO researchers unearthed the fact that some units attempted to
solve this problem by getting civilian doctors to conduct physical examinations. While expedient, this solution had a drawback; the
civilian physicians, unfamiliar with Army requirements, sometimes
submitted reports that did not meet prescribed standards. Poorly
trained civilian clerks, hired to cope with a shortage of clerical
assistance, made errors that contributed to delays in processing of
physical examination records.

Reserve units suffered from a general lack of administrative and
supply personnel so important to the alert, movement, and processing
of large numbers of troops. HERO evaluates the reserve units' personnel in these categories as "inexperienced, insufficiently trained in
specialities," and, in the case of the National Guard, "unfamiliar
with Army regulations and procedures." HERO finds that "there was
a general lack of supply, maintenance, [and] technical manuals,
regulations, and forms in National Guard units. . . . Supply channels for clothing and housekeeping items badly needed in the
shakedown period did not function adequately for nearly two months
after units arrived at training stations. Advance parties sent by divisions to training posts did not include sufficient service troops to
prepare ration breakdown, communications, medical facilities, construction, and maintenance shops."[13]

Once at training stations, inductees underwent classification processing that, were it not for the inexperience of unit administrative personnel, could have been done earlier. The Army sent processing teams
to the centers to aid in the preparation of records. There were delays
while the teams instructed unit personnel in the techniques of
classification.

Other Regular Army teams on temporary duty at the centers provided special precycle training for some officers and noncommissioned officers. This program, which HERO describes as "fairly successful," sought to prepare the personnel who would form essential
cadres. There was a trade-off involved, however. Time spent on individual subjects meant the disruption of training within small
units—a failing that had to be made up later. The HERO study also

---

[13]HERO, "Mobilization in the Korean Conflict," pp. 45-46.

notes that mobilized units sent hundreds of officers and enlisted men to Regular Army service schools in their initial eight weeks on active duty. Unit commanders hoped—and it seemed a reasonable expectation—that increased efficiency resulting from this training would more than balance the inevitable blow that the trainees' absence dealt to unit cohesion. But success here required careful selection of those to be trained, and in HERO's view the training quotas in many cases were allotted too quickly to permit judicious screening of candidates.

Another difficulty that the HERO study treats is the staggered arrivals of selective service fillers for National Guard units at the training stations. Thousands of these men scheduled to join each division within a brief period instead came in dribs and drabs over periods ranging up to six weeks. The start of basic training for the units was delayed concomitantly.

When training got under way, shortages of equipment hampered it. Because of the situation in the Far East and the Army's expansion, equipment was not plentiful anywhere, but it was perhaps most scarce, according to HERO, in recalled reserve units. Many of these units were equipped largely with World War II items and even then at a very low percentage of what was authorized. Most commonly in short supply were vehicles, weapons, and engineering, communications, and maintenance equipment. Partly the shortages stemmed from transfers of equipment from the reserve components to the active Army, which had very immediate needs for it. Kendall gives transfer figures, for the war's first year, of 750 tanks and 5,600 other vehicles from the National Guard. HERO's "Mobilization" states that items withdrawn from both the guard and the organized reserve through April 1951 included approximately 100 liaison aircraft, 150 medium tanks, 7,000 other vehicles, 1,000 recoilless rifles, 250 4.2-inch mortars, and 2,250 radios.

To cope with the general shortages, the Army early in 1951 established a minimum equipment distribution policy. All units were to receive a full issue of small arms, medical supplies, and individual clothing and equipment. TOE units were to get only 30 percent of their authorized allowances of organizational equipment upon activation and then 50 percent after four months' training. Full allowances would come only upon receipt of alert orders or a directive for movement overseas. HERO states that many units could not reach even these levels in the first half of 1951 and judges that allowances under the minimum equipment distribution program proved inadequate for training purposes in critical categories such as signal and ordnance items, and vehicles. Stilwaugh's "Personnel Policies in the Korean Conflict" makes clear that the Army would have been unable to call up more National Guard units than it did with any reasonable hope of supplying them with equipment.

Beset by equipment problems, the reserve components also had to deal with a diminution of unit integrity. HERO notes that this was a difficulty particularly for nondivisional units, activated in the first wave of recalls, that lacked the time to achieve a cohesive unit identity or undergo a balanced training program. Kendall examines the situation of support units, which were badly understrength when recalled at the beginning of the war. He notes that when these units proved a drain on scarce training facilities, the Army's solution was to deactivate them and use their men as individual replacements—a move that predictably angered the reserve components. Levies on reserve units to provide fillers for the Far East Command in 1951 produced, the HERO study observes, a considerable decline in the efficiency of the units levied. Stilwaugh discusses objectively the dilemma that the principle of unit integrity created: at what point was the need to protect that integrity outweighed by the personnel demands in the theater of operations?

Besides the integrity of activated units, national policy makers had to consider the integrity as a mobilization reserve of that part of the civilian components not activated. Prewar planners had not provided for the eventuality of a partial activation of reserves and the concurrent need to retain a capability for response to a larger emergency, as HERO's "Mobilization" points out. HERO concludes that with only 40 percent of the organized reserve's strength mobilized and 34 percent of the guard's, the requirements of the situation were met—even if hurried arrangements did not produce the most efficient use of manpower. This conclusion seems to beg the question: how well would the reserves have been able to meet a greater emergency?

From the point of view of the states, another danger was the potential inability of state governments to respond to emergencies within their borders if most of their National Guard forces had been federalized to deal with the Korean War. HERO's "US Home Defense Forces Study" (prepared for the Office of the Assistant Secretary of Defense, 1979) gives a detailed explanation of how the states dealt with this situation in both world wars and the Korean War. A variety of local solutions sufficed for the comparatively brief duration of World War I, but World War II required larger and more systematic efforts. State forces developed during the second war maintained a mustered strength of 150,000 to 200,000 and ably filled in for the guard in providing routine internal security duties. Looking to that experience, the military authorities in the states in mid-1950 began to prepare plans for the reintroduction of state guards. The states could begin organization and enlist cadres under state laws, but they could not begin active organization without federal legislative authority for the establishment of state forces and for the provision of federal arms and equipment. Congress passed authorizing legislation late in September 1950, but most states awaited the development of federal policies that would determine how much money and equipment they would receive. Because a total mobilization of the National Guard could not be ruled out as the war wore on, the National Guard Bureau planned to assist the states in a full-scale organization of state forces in that eventuality—but only in that eventuality. Since only about a third of the guard units were mobilized, the bureau never implemented the plan. As a result, few states went very far in active organization of units. The Army sought to alleviate the internal security fears of states whose guard units were overseas through the selective stationing of military police battalions.

In the latter part of 1950, the Army was too preoccupied with mobilization of the reserve forces to pay a great deal of attention to the concerns of the states about home guards. By October 1950, having gotten through the initial, crucial phase of recalls and activations, the Army could devote attention to solving the serious procedural problems that had emerged in the first few months of the war. HERO's "Mobilization" recounts the Army's announcement in that month of a new policy under which those involuntarily recalled would receive at least four months' notification before having to report for duty. The HERO study goes on to detail the Army's attempts to improve the activation process for recalled units. Like recalled individuals, units would get four months' notice. Revised regulations provided for standardized induction and movement orders and for improved methods of coordination between echelons. The Department of Defense promulgated uniform policies on deferments.

The large-scale intervention in the war by the People's Republic of China in November 1950 shifted the Army's attention from procedural improvements to an accelerated expansion of its forces. Planners hoped to mobilize six more National Guard divisions from January to March 1951 but had to postpone that schedule to June to October 1951 due to a lack of sufficient equipment for training.

Without a total industrial mobilization, the HERO study observes, those divisions could not be combat-ready and fully supported until well into 1952.

Pressure to enlarge the Army, HERO notes, led to backsliding on some of the fall 1950 reforms of mobilization procedures. The proposed alert period of four months fell by the wayside in January 1951, when the notification period was reduced to thirty days. Although General Clark had recommended that unit members requiring special training be inducted in advance of their units, the thirty-day alert period was simply too short to conduct such training. Activated units in the first six months of 1951, therefore, found themselves reduced in many cases to one officer per company, while the rest of the officers underwent special instruction. This situation, according to HERO's "Mobilization," produced a marked effect on the training capabilities of the units.

There was one success, HERO finds, in the activations early in 1951. Two specially trained eleven-man teams from the Adjutant General's Corps eased the adjustments of National Guard units to Army procedures.

On the other hand, the time spent in personnel processing after activation was still excessive. The key to this difficulty, the HERO study relates, was the National Guard's continuing refusal to adopt the Army personnel record system. If the guard, when not on active duty, employed this system, processing could be completed before mobilization. National Guard officials countered that not only was the current system adequate, but also the proposed switch might violate existing legislation. Further, guard units lacked both the trained personnel and the training time to convert. In the final National Guard activations in early 1952, The Adjutant General attempted to alleviate the problem of dual record systems by having the guard units prepare in advance some of the information needed for the completion of personnel forms. The HERO study judges this effort a failure, primarily because the military districts and the units lacked the manpower necessary to do the work properly and completely.

Selective Service

After the Regular Army and the civilian components were tapped as sources of military manpower, the draft came next. The Selective Service Act of 24 June 1948 required men from eighteen to twenty-six years old to register, and set the term of service at twenty-one months.

Congress limited the life of the law to two years. Kendall credits the act with two accomplishments before the Korean War: by registering and classifying men, it reduced the time needed to mobilize when the war erupted; and, through the threat of induction, it maintained the strength of the Army and the civilian components at the budgetary level.

In *Lewis B. Hershey, Mr. Selective Service* (Chapel Hill: University of North Carolina Press, 1985), George Q. Flynn shows that extension of the draft in an active form, rather than in a standby status with little selective service machinery, was in doubt just before the North Korean invasion late in June 1950. The emergency brought a quick extension of the law from Congress, but only for one year. Having had a small budget, the Selective Service System in Washington was not very well prepared for Korea. But, as Flynn demonstrates, Maj. Gen. Lewis B. Hershey headed an organization designed to operate on a decentralized basis with strong local participation in decision making. As a result, the system did not experience difficulty in meeting the Army's manpower requirements in 1950.

There was little use in drafting men unless they could be trained promptly, and Kendall and HERO's "Mobilization" both discuss impediments to rapid training. Only months before the war, the Army had reduced the number of its training camps; it now had to reverse the procedure. Equipment, treated above, was another limiting factor. Regular Army cadres that ordinarily would have directed training were in, or headed for, Korea as replacements. National Guard divisions therefore trained the initial inductees, while ORC officers organized the new training facilities that had to be set up.

When the Chinese intervened in Korea, draft calls shot up. Hershey, Flynn relates, took the opportunity to seek an indefinite extension of selective service, an expansion of the age liability, and an increase in the mandated period of service for draftees, in addition to a reduction in deferments. The resurgence of United Nations forces and the subsequent stalemate in Korea tended to blunt somewhat the urgency of the selective service director's pleas, but Congress in June 1951 did establish the system on a permanent basis (albeit with induction authority limited to four years), lower the draft age, and increase the term of service.

By the time of the passage of the selective service extension, draft calls had decreased because of the improved military situation. (Flynn dramatically refers also to President Truman's attempt to "drag General MacArthur back from the brink of all-out war with

China.")[14] Still, the calls were quite large. Kendall provides some figures: 340,000 men required for the first six months of 1951, a quota that selective service exceeded by 25,000. For the remainder of the year, the Army asked for only 143,000. With the pool of men classified I-A (available for immediate induction) depleted, Hershey paradoxically faced a tighter situation than in the first half of the year, when calls had been more than twice as great. The culprit, Flynn and Kendall agree, was deferments. A liberal deferment policy gave the lie to claims that there was a surplus of manpower, even in a partial mobilization.

Flynn deals with another very important point about the overall thrust of the draft. During World War II, the United States abandoned the enlistment of volunteers, primarily because of the havoc created by indiscriminate removals of workers from the economy and also because the unpredictability of volunteering posed a problem for draft call estimates. In the Korean War, the government retained the enlistment option, thereby placing selective service in the role of a goad to volunteering. Flynn faults the Department of Defense for supporting volunteering as a money-saver—a claim he disputes, citing the cost of recruitment—and for concealing the real motive for the policy, which was to "skim off the cream of the manpower supply before it became diluted in the vat of draftees."[15]

Replacements

By means of extraordinary shuffling of his own forces, recounted above, General MacArthur managed to get enough troops to the combat zone to meet the North Korean challenge of June 1950. That was but the beginning. Possessing only a rudimentary replacement system, the Far East Command had to establish a theater organization to provide replacements both for the Eighth Army in Korea and for the skeletonized 7th Division in Japan. In July the command set up a replacement training center at Yokohama and a replacement training battalion at Sasebo, Japan, and another replacement battalion at Pusan, South Korea. According to HERO's "Analytic Survey of Personnel Replacement Systems in Modern War" (prepared for the U.S. Army TRADOC Systems Analysis Activity, April 1981, and hereafter cited as HERO's "Analytic Survey"), the installations in Japan processed 38,000 replacements, over 70 percent of whom were moved by

---

[14]Flynn, *Lewis B. Hershey*, p. 181.
[15]Ibid., p. 185.

air, between 17 July and 30 September 1950. Air movement of replacements on that scale was an innovation.

In mid-August MacArthur requested that reservists be transferred immediately from the United States to his command as replacements. The Office of the Chief of Army Field Forces agreed but insisted that the recalled reservists first receive three weeks of refresher training. In actuality, reports HERO's "Mobilization," processing to meet shipping deadlines shaved significant time from this three-week period for many reservists.

Few things in mobilization happen immediately, and this was true of the effect of draftees on the military situation in late 1950. Even after the initial inductions resulting from the operations of the Selective Service System in September, Kendall notes, the length of time required to train the new soldiers meant no quick relief for General MacArthur. Kendall states that General Clark, facing a lag of six months between induction and the provision of replacements, slashed basic training from fourteen to six weeks. This assertion overstates the reduction of training time, since Clark also increased the length of the training week. Nevertheless, this August reduction was significant and, as Kendall says, may have resulted in poorly trained troops and consequently greater casualties.

Then, the tremendous success of United Nations forces at Inchon and subsequent impressive advances brought a period of considerable optimism. For the next two months, the United States planned for a reduction of its forces in the Far East. The sudden shift in fortunes when the Chinese entered the war in November meant that replacement schedules, which had been pared to conform with the bright outlook, had to be changed again. Time was lost as a result.

HERO's "Mobilization" discusses the detrimental effects that replacement levies wrought in the first half of 1951 on activated civilian component units, especially those of the National Guard. When guard units had newly trained specialists snatched from them, readiness and morale plummeted. The need to train fresh fillers in the units meant that different parts of divisions were at different stages of training at any given time. Training schedules lengthened. With the difficulties that the Selective Service System had in meeting draft calls in the second half of the year, the Army remained, Kendall says, "critically short of replacements for its multiple manpower missions."[16]

---

[16]Kendall, "Inflexible Response,"p. 224.

For the first nine months of the war, the Far East Command complained not only of insufficient numbers of replacements, but also of the soldierly quality of those received. Above all else, General MacArthur needed men in the combat arms. A large proportion—60 percent through January 1951—of those he received were service troops. The Army was sending what it could muster. Many of the men were not physically fit to carry out strenuous duties in the rugged Korean terrain. Commanders in Korea found the state of their training poor. Seven to ten days of refresher training and physical conditioning often were necessary before replacements could go into the line. Stilwaugh, who discusses these problems, finds that they eased after the Eighth Army began receiving draftees in March 1951. Ironically, in view of the surfeit of service troops, the theater history, "Logistics in the Korean Operations," relates the complaint of service units that they suffered a chronic shortage of certain types of specialists. The history does state, however, that "the availability of replacements had no significant impact on the logistical operations during the Korean conflict."[17]

Rotation

Hand in hand with replacement policies went a system of rotation. Stilwaugh cites General Clark's realization, early in the war, that the maintenance of troop morale necessitated a policy for rotating men out of Korea. There was also homefront morale—that of relatives and friends of the troops—to consider. If a small proportion of young men had to fight the war indefinitely, with no planned rotation from the combat zone, public and congressional pressure for relief could be expected. Moreover, World War II had demonstrated that sustained combat eventually tended to make some soldiers careless, overconfident, or indifferent. Military expediency and simple humanity added weight to arguments for rotation.

Delayed for months by Chinese entrance into the war, a rotation system finally went into effect in April 1951. Stilwaugh and the theater history describe the criteria for eligibility. Troops with six months in combat or twelve months in the rear areas of Korea were available for rotation—whether or not, according to the theater history, the Army had replacements for them. Under this plan, 3,765 officers and 77,383 enlisted men returned to the United States. Two important flaws in the system soon became obvious, reports

---

[17]"Logistics in the Korean Operations," vol. I, frame 1183. (References to this study are from the microfilm copy in the Center of Military History.)

Stilwaugh. First, the Army lacked the men to support as rapid a turnover as the policy required. Second, the Army had not made sufficiently clear to the troops that eligibility did not guarantee rotation, that going home actually depended on the arrival of a replacement for the individual soldier. Therefore, many men remained in Korea past the allotted time and felt that they were being discriminated against. There is an obvious discrepancy here between Stilwaugh and the theater history over the role of replacements in the implementation of the April policy.

On 21 July 1951 the Army instituted a revised rotation plan. Soldiers now accumulated "constructive months' service" according to the nature and length of their assignments in the Far East Command. A month in combat equaled four constructive months, a month in Korea but not in combat was worth two constructive months, and, lest troops elsewhere be forgotten, a month in other parts of the command earned one-and-a-half months of constructive credit. The total credits necessary to qualify for rotation varied from month to month, depending on the Army's forecast of the number of replacements that would be available. Stilwaugh describes other details of the plan, particularly intratheater rotation, that aimed at easing the soldier's lot, but does not make clear whether the uncertainty engendered by the second plan was actually a great improvement over that endured under the first version.

Rotation involved problems not easily solved. Kendall and Stilwaugh treat the complication stemming from the need to release involuntarily recalled reservists at the end of their legally mandated service in 1951. These releases meant that the Far East Command required many more replacements; rotation slowed accordingly. Line units in Korea inevitably suffered from the rotation of seasoned officers and enlisted leaders. By removing trained specialists, Stilwaugh notes, the rotation program forced the Far East Command to increase the number of men in its specialist schools. This training removed men from combat units and reduced unit effectiveness while they were gone. Kendall observes that an attempt to alleviate this difficulty through levies on National Guard divisions in the United States sacrificed the readiness of the units levied. HERO's "Analytic Survey" renders a mixed verdict on the rotation system. "Rotation became an effective tool in maintaining the spirit of US troops in the sporadic defensive warfare of 1952–1953 in which boredom and the alien land and climate of the theater of operations sapped morale. There can be no doubt, however, that the very thoroughness and scale of the program contributed to a general lowering of Eighth Army combat efficiency. This was a trade-off the Army could afford during a period of static warfare."[18]

An alternative method of rotating soldiers out of Korea, and one that seemed to some Army planners to be more efficient, was unit rotation. Stilwaugh devotes considerable attention to the pros and cons of this method and finds many advantages. National Guard units, composed of men from particular geographic areas, would experience a salutary boost in pride if they could fight together. In general, the efficiency of units would increase because men who trained and then fought alongside one another would have higher morale; there would be greater unit cohesion. For commanders, the concept would offer predictability about troop turnover. On the minus side, unit rotation would require one unit training in the United States to take the place of each unit in Korea—an extravagant use of manpower in view of limited budgets imposed on the Army. Stilwaugh concludes that "although the Department of the Army and all the lower echelons appeared to agree that unit rotation was attractive, practical, that it would produce better leadership among officers and noncommissioned officers and would foster esprit de corps, one simple and inescapable fact prevented the Army from putting it into practice during the Korean Conflict. The Army could not afford it."[19]

Twice during the war, the Army did employ unit rotation successfully and with large units. Hermes' *Truce Tent and Fighting Front* relates how the National Guard's 45th and 40th Infantry Divisions relieved the 1st Cavalry and 24th Infantry Divisions, respectively, from the line in Korea in December 1951 and January 1952. Based on the later performance of the two guard divisions, the Eighth Army G-3 judged them to be equal in combat effectiveness to the divisions they had replaced. (There may be an element of damning with faint praise in this evaluation, since the 1st Cavalry and 24th Infantry Divisions had suffered from the loss of experienced soldiers under the individual rotation program.)

Korea, Europe, and Planning

Shortly before the dispatch of the two National Guard divisions to Korea, the 28th and 43d Infantry Divisions, also guard units, had embarked for Europe. Two Regular Army divisions, the 4th Infantry and the 2d Armored, had deployed to Europe in the summer of 1951.

---

[18]HERO, "Analytic Survey," p. 146.
[19]Stilwaugh, "Personnel Policies in the Korean Conflict," frame 599.

These deployments indicated the duality of the problem that confronted U.S. planners throughout the war: the aggression in Korea had to be contained while the United States attempted to guard against a thrust against Western Europe by the Soviet Union. In a partial mobilization, with the nation not geared economically or psychologically to all-out war, the resources that the United States could bring to this two-sided task were limited.

Kendall reveals the depths of the dilemma in discussing the effects of Chinese entry into the war in November 1950. With an eye toward Europe, the Joint Chiefs of Staff began planning for withdrawal from Korea. This drastic step did not become necessary, but the Army was unable to meet General MacArthur's request in mid-December for the dispatch of four National Guard divisions to Japan. HERO's "Mobilization" recounts the Army G–3's observation that, for psychological reasons, a movement of divisions to Japan would have to be accompanied by a corresponding movement to Europe. Subsequent deployment decisions reflected this line of reasoning.

Manpower was not the only element in the dilemma. Huston's "Korean Logistics" treats the concomitant concern with supplies. After the outbreak of war in Korea, the Army sought to maintain a rough balance in supply priorities between that conflict and Europe—an especially difficult task in the early stages of the war. In addition, the continuing requirements of the Korean War had to be weighed against the need to build up reserve stocks of material for a possible future war of greater magnitude and scope.

These tasks were even more trying because of the repeated assumption by U.S. policy makers, for planning purposes, that the Korean War would end in six months. Huston is severely critical of "the over-optimism of high-level officials who insisted on assigning dates no more than six to twelve months in advance by which hostilities were supposed to end." Seeking the cause of this optimism, he finds that "it was not clear whether this policy sprang mainly from an anxiety to avoid the accumulation of another stockpile of surplus property, or from a studied consideration that this was best for the American economy and military position, or whether it emanated from a desire to meet criticism by maintaining an appearance of economical operations marked by an attitude of *'Apres moi le deluge.'* What was clear was the crippling effect which that policy had on effective logistic support."[20]

---

[20]Huston, "Korean Logistics," ch. VI, p. 36.

Huston makes allowance for optimism up to November 1950 but faults policy makers for failing to change their assessment in light of battlefield events. He questions

the continuation of such assumptions in the midst of all-out Chinese counterattacks. Throughout the first half of 1951 — even when General MacArthur was doubting the ability of the United Nations to keep a foothold in Korea — the official Department of Defense assumption remained that hostilities would end by 30 June 1951. This meant that no supplies could be purchased for a conflict in Korea continuing after that date. Since order and shipping time to Korea was 120 days, in March supplies being shipped for support of operations after 30 June had to be obtained by further depletion of depot stocks and by diversion of production which had been intended for other world-wide commitments. Although G-4, in March 1951, recommended that the Department of Defense assume the continuation of combat in Korea, no action resulted. Not until 29 June 1951, by which time it had become clear even to the most casual observer that the Korean war probably would not end the next day, the Secretary of Defense extended the assumed termination date.[21]

Stilwaugh and Kendall make similar, if somewhat less sharp, criticisms in regard to the effects of the same assumptions on manpower.

Moving Troops to Korea

Once decisions on resources for Korea were made, and the resources — troops and materiel — were in hand, the next step was to assemble and transport them to Korea.[22] Although some replacements went by air, most went by water. Huston takes a close look at the feverish preparations for movement of the 2d Infantry Division from the United States in the first weeks of the war. To deploy the division as fast as possible, the Army General Staff had to streamline and accelerate its normal procedures. Regulations governing preparations for overseas movement had to be modified. Trimming a process that normally took two weeks, G-4 prepared and dispatched in three days an abbreviated movement directive for the 2d Division. Technical service representatives at Fort Lewis, Washington, the division's assembly point, made requisitions for equipment by telephone instead of waiting for paper work to go through. To bring the division up to strength for deployment, the Army stripped other units. Transportation of these men to Fort Lewis was haphazard, with some arriving tardily in privately owned vehicles.

---

[21]Ibid., pp. 36-37.
[22]Transportation of materiel will be treated in the section on distribution.

The commander of the 2d Division wanted his units combat loaded, with troops and their equipment on the same ships and placed so that they could be unloaded quickly and ready for combat. This method required more space than other shipping methods, and sufficient bottoms were not immediately available. Since time was of the essence, the division commander settled for a compromise of unit loading. Under this system, as much unit equipment as possible went on the ships with the troops, with the remainder sailing on cargo ships scheduled to arrive simultaneously.

On 17 July 1950 the first elements of the 2d Division sailed for Japan, where the division was to be staged for transport to Korea. A change in plans brought these troops directly to Korea, where they arrived on 31 July. The last elements of the division reached the port of Pusan on 20 August. Huston praises this movement as the fastest transport of a combat division overseas in U.S. history.

Korean Augmentation to the U.S. Army

Desperate for replacements early in August 1950, General MacArthur authorized the Eighth Army to augment its strength with Korean manpower. This expedient soon became formalized through conferences with the Republic of Korea (ROK) Army. Dubbed Korean Army Troops, U.S. Army (KATUSA), the program called for the integration of South Korean soldiers into U.S. units, with the ROK Army retaining responsibility for their administration, pay, and discipline.

Stilwaugh supplies a detailed and judicious account of the KATUSA program. She reports that the 7th Infantry Division, which received the first of 8,600 Koreans in mid-August 1950, found staggering problems in their use. Knowledge of the English language, military training, and equipment were all practically nonexistent among the "augmentees." Because of the shortness of time, only two weeks' training with U.S. troops was possible before the division landed at Inchon in mid-September. Other U.S. divisions in Korea received an initial allotment of 250 Koreans each and found them likewise totally unprepared for combat. The ROK Army, badly mauled and confused in the early stages of the war, was simply impressing men off the streets of Korean cities to meet KATUSA quotas. These bewildered "recruits" went directly to U.S. units. Although the Eighth Army soon established four training centers for KATUSA personnel, some in the initial augmentations went directly into combat without training because of the seriousness of the military situation.

American commanders found much to complain about in their new Korean troops. The inability of the Army to supply a sufficient number of translators made control of the Koreans in combat almost impossible. Nor could the men be adequately trained in the technical aspects of weapons and gunnery. Their habits of personal hygiene and field sanitation left a great deal to be desired by American standards. Control of discipline by the ROK Army meant undesirable delays between infractions and punishment. Used to a diet of rice, lower in calories but higher in bulk than American rations, the Koreans seemed to be complaining constantly of hunger. Diminutive in size compared to Americans, they were difficult to fit with U.S. uniforms. Stilwaugh notes also, in what may be an understatement, that "some U.S. soldiers were unable to adjust themselves to a situation in which the South Koreans were equal partners in the same organization."[23]

Originally, the developers of the KATUSA program planned that each U.S. division would get 8,300 Korean augmentees. Except for the 7th and 3d Infantry Divisions, the number of Koreans per division was hardly ever greater than 3,000. As Stilwaugh notes, the ROK Army had enough trouble filling its own manpower needs, let alone those of the Eighth Army. In addition to this difficulty, the sour experience of many U.S. commanders with their Korean troops resulted in a reduction of KATUSA soldiers in American units in the fall of 1950, as more U.S. replacements became available. KATUSA strength peaked at 27,369 in mid-November of that year. Much later, in mid-1952, the combination of release of reservists, combat rotation, and tight budgets dictated an increase in Korean augmentees from a level of about 10,000 to an authorized level of 20,000.

Stilwaugh is not entirely negative in her appraisal of the KATUSA program. She appreciates their usefulness in artillery and service units. Artillery was an adaptable function for them because many commands could be relayed easily by visual means. Many of the Koreans proved to be good welders, automobile mechanics, and maintenance men, and they performed adequately as wiremen and guards in signal units. An area in which they shone was the handling of refugees. In addition, they were much better than their American comrades at distinguishing between North and South Koreans during night operations. While acknowledging the generally unsatisfactory record of KATUSA personnel in combat in 1950, Stilwaugh points out that Koreans who remained with U.S. units developed into accept-

---

[23]Stilwaugh, "Personnel Policies in the Korean Conflict," frame 666.

Advance detachment of the 71st Signal Service Battalion, part of the Pusan Base Command, undergoes an inspection.

Stripped to their shorts, members of the first group of New York City draftees wait for their physical examinations at the Army's main recruiting station, 18 July 1950.

Inductees are sworn into the Army at the Induction Center in Baltimore, Maryland.

Arrival of the one millionth man to be handled through the port of Pusan by a unit of the 2d Logistical Command, 6 August 1951.

Trainees of Battery C, 43d Field Artillery Battalion, listening to a lecture at Fort Jackson, South Carolina, on abbreviations used in signal communications.

At Fort Jackson, South Carolina, incoming inductees pass troops bound for Korea.

Trainees at Fort Jackson, South Carolina, receive instructions on the use of the recoilless rifle.

Two soldiers of the 323d Engineer Company, U.S. IX Corps, wait happily outside the rotation office for the papers that will send them home from Korea.

323 ENGR
L E CO
ROTATION PLAN
ROTATE HERE

Veterans of the fighting in Korea sit in an LST that will take them to a homebound ship.

Cross-section of the troop compartment aboard the USS *Pickaway*, a troopship transporting personnel of the U.S. 24th Infantry Division from Korea to Japan, 11 February 1952.

Members of the 23d Infantry, 2d Infantry Division, on the pier after debarking from a ship at Pusan, 6 August 1950.

Troops of the 17th Infantry Division land at Inchon Harbor aboard LSTs, 18 September 1950.

able combat soldiers after sufficient experience and training. In general, she provides a reminder that "these simple people with a background that was primarily agricultural suddenly found themselves confronted with the complexities of a modern war machine."[24]

In *South to the Naktong, North to the Yalu,* Appleman is more completely negative in his evaluation of the KATUSA experience, on the basis of roughly the same type of evidence as Stilwaugh's. This difference of opinion probably is attributable to Appleman's focus on combat activities and to his narrower chronological scope; he considers the KATUSA program only in the context of "August Build-Up and September Portents" (his chapter title) in 1950.

Taking a broader look in "The KATUSA Experiment: The Integration of Korean Nationals into the U.S. Army, 1950–1965," *Military Affairs* 38 (April 1974), David Curtis Skaggs states without equivocation that "as a source of filler troops for under-manned American units being sent into combat, the KATUSA program was a complete failure." Skaggs does find other positive aspects in the program, however, in addition to those adduced by Stilwaugh. The KATUSA troops, unlike their American counterparts, never rotated out of the theater. As a result, "their battlefield experience made them the seasoned veterans that every well-functioning combat unit needs."[25] And from the American perspective, the Korean augmentees had the advantage of lowering American casualties—the more Koreans in the front line, the fewer Americans who had to be there.

Industrial Mobilization and Procurement

While commanders in Korea coped with their manpower problems, U.S. officials at home had to develop policies that would provide the physical wherewithal to carry on the war. Yoshpe's *A Case Study in Peacetime Mobilization Planning* supplies some detail on the activities of the National Security Resources Board in this regard. Yoshpe's monograph is perhaps most important for its treatment of the first six months of the war, when the board had the responsibility for overall coordination of mobilization. Reinforcing the NSRB's advisory role, President Truman in September 1950 designated the agency's chairman as his staff agent for overall coordination of the defense effort. The president also charged the chairman with specific operating functions in financial areas such as tax amortization and

---

[24]Ibid., frame 674.
[25]Skaggs, "The KATUSA Experiment," p. 55.

loans for defense contractors. Truman's actions were in keeping with his intention to carry out a partial mobilization with a minimum number of emergency agencies.

The NSRB's strategy was to expand the economy with the fewest possible controls to meet defense needs, rather than simply shifting some current civilian production to defense purposes. Yoshpe explains that this approach was validated by the Defense Production Act of September 1950, which provided for a rearmament program geared not as much to the Korean emergency as to the establishment of an industrial base capable of handling an all-out war. Vawter's *Industrial Mobilization* ties this policy to the key National Security Council paper, NSC 68, which in early 1950 posited the need for the United States to prepare to meet expected large-scale Soviet aggression within the next few years. (Rearden's *The Formative Years* contains a good discussion of the origins and content of NSC 68.)

Lacking sufficient information on military requirements and beset by a general weakness in relation to other agencies, the National Security Resources Board was not effective in the coordination and planning of military procurement. Yoshpe reveals that there were no developed plans for procurement as late as mid-December 1950. Following the massive Chinese intervention in Korea, President Truman on 16 December proclaimed the existence of a national emergency and created the Office of Defense Mobilization. To this office and its subsidiary Defense Production Administration, established in January 1951, the president transferred the NSRB's coordinating function, leaving that agency with little more than its own operating functions. Neither Yoshpe nor Vawter explains Truman's decision, although some of the reasons behind it can be inferred from Yoshpe's description of the NSRB's tribulations in the first six months of the war.

In "Korean Logistics," Huston credits Truman's declaration of emergency with easing constraints on Army procurement. The Army could now make contracts without advertising for competitive bids. Further, the under secretary of the Army could delegate to subordinates the responsibility for approving many contracts that he previously had had to approve himself.

A major emphasis of Huston's, in dealing with industrial mobilization and procurement, is on Army policy makers' concern that the Chinese intervention would trigger too large a mobilization. Here again, the theme is building for a larger war while meeting the emergency of Korea. Army officials feared that a full mobilization, with the requirement to supply large numbers of new troops, would strain productive capacity while simultaneously taking industry's skilled workers in the draft. The result could be a serious blow to the intended gradual buildup for a possible larger conflict.

Vawter outlines the tasks and issues that faced industrial mobilization officials throughout the war. He pictures 1951 as a year of tooling up and preparing for full-scale military production. A major bottleneck in this process was a shortage in some geographical areas of engineers, designers, and draftsmen. Another was an inadequate output of machine tools. Whether to strive for quantity or quality in war materiel and how to deal with long lead times for complex weapons—these were issues that would continue to confront policy makers for many years to come. After an accelerated buildup in 1952, the rate of production of important items was significantly higher by 1953. This process raised the possibility that some programs would soon be completed, thus leaving a "cold" production base. Always with an eye to the long range, officials decided to stretch out production of tanks and wheeled vehicles, among many other items.

For the historian concerned with the mobilization, equipping, and supplying of troops, the production of specific items of equipment is the most relevant aspect of industrial mobilization. There is virtually no sustained treatment in the literature on the Korean War of the production of individual items, with the exception of ammunition. Had it not been for a controversial shortage of ammunition during the war, the details surrounding this particular item probably would have remained, like the rest, available only in the archives.

Hermes' *Truce Tent and Fighting Front* aptly refers to "the perplexing and tortuous labyrinth of ammunition shortages."[26] In April 1953 the Preparedness Subcommittee No. 2 of the Senate Armed Services Committee held nine days of hearings on "Ammunition Shortages in the Armed Services," (83d Cong., 1st sess., 1953). The result was over seven hundred pages of printed testimony and related material. Maj. Gen. William O. Reeder, Assistant Deputy Chief of Staff, G-4, for most of the war, later commented that the hearings did not present the facts in a particularly coherent fashion. As a partial remedy, Reeder produced his own detailed account, "The Korean Ammunition Shortage," (c. 1955, copy in the Center of Military History). Reeder's study, in turn, is ably summarized in Hermes' *Truce Tent and Fighting Front.*

---

[26]Hermes, *Truce Tent and Fighting Front,* p. 224.

Reeder emphasizes the importance of the state of the ammunition stockpile left from World War II. Although tremendous in toto, the inventory was seriously unbalanced, with only small amounts of important types of rounds, such as 155-mm. Training in the late 1940s consumed ammunition that the Army did not try seriously to replace. Economy in defense expenditures and lack of enough personnel to conduct a comprehensive inventory did not help matters. By June 1950, the stockpile was by far the Army's major source of ammunition, since most World War II producers had long since reconverted to civilian production.

Even after the beginning of the Korean War, complacency born of the size of the stockpile, combined with the expectation of a short war and the desire for a gradual buildup of the industrial base, delayed the mobilization of ammunition producers. Sobered by the shock of Chinese entrance, Congress in January 1951 made its first large ammunition appropriation. Lead time for most items of production, however, was eighteen to twenty-four months, which meant that the weight of production would not be felt until late in 1952 at best.

On the battlefield, conditions contributed to what became a public perception of a serious ammunition shortage. Hermes comments on the effect of the great reduction in the number of artillery battalions per corps, compared to World War II corps. He quotes the observation of General James A. Van Fleet, Eighth Army commander, that "the effectiveness of one volley from four battalions is far greater than four volleys from one battalion."[27] Ammunition expenditure was correspondingly greater. The static war that developed in mid-1951 meant heavier use of artillery, which in turn caused an increase in the day of supply (average number of rounds fired daily) for ammunition. Pressure on the reserve stocks grew. The Army had to reduce the rate of daily fire in the winter and spring of 1952, which brought complaints from soldiers in Korea and eventually a great deal of public and congressional concern.

Hermes concludes—and Huston agrees—that the shortages that existed on the front were temporary and that the Eighth Army could always use whatever ammunition it needed to protect itself. Hermes also points out that Eighth Army artillery fire consistently exceeded that of the enemy. Reeder, Hermes, and Huston are unanimous in their belief that the real shortage was not in Korea but in the Army's

---

[27]Ibid., p. 228.

total resources of ammunition in relation to its worldwide commitments. As always, the specter of a war in Europe proved the measure for Army capabilities.

In the early months of the Korean War, Huston notes, supply from the United States could not meet all the needs of the Far East Command. Luckily for the troops in the combat zone, there were large quantities of equipment in Japan that were left over from World War II. In 1945 the United States had begun a "roll-up" operation to collect materiel all over the Pacific but was forced to halt it because of demobilization. The Far East Command began another roll-up in 1947 to support U.S. occupation forces in Japan. As a result, large quantities of equipment were collected in Japan, and the Army began an ordnance rebuild program. When the Korean War started, the Army pushed for a great increase in the program; whereas in the first half of 1950 production in Japan had been about 3,000 rebuilt vehicles, in the last six months of the year 28,000 came off the lines. Of the many vehicles that moved from Japan to Korea in those first six months of the war, a high percentage were from the rebuild program or from overhaul operations: of 26,000 general-purpose vehicles, 70 percent; of 787 tanks, 45 percent; and of 1,900 other combat vehicles, 82 percent. By May 1951 the Army employed 30,000 Japanese on rebuild work. A year later the number of general-purpose vehicles rebuilt in Japan was nearing 100,000. Huston believes that the program probably saved the tactical situation in Korea, and he lays considerable stress on the large savings—by some accounts over $9 billion—that it produced.

But even with this crucial supplement to supply from the United States, Huston observes, there still was a gap between requirements and shipments arriving in the combat zone. Much of this deficit the United States was able to make up with purchases in Japan. Rope, lumber, sandbags, dynamite, gasoline drums, railway equipment, and various other items were all available on the Japanese market. Although U.S. purchases in Korea were considerable, Korean industry was more primitive than that in Japan. Huston ponders the negative consequences if the emergency in 1950 had been in Indochina or Iran, both of which lacked a nearby available industrial base such as that which Japan provided for Korea.

Logistical Organization

But the war was in Korea and it spread no further. Unlike the two world wars, this one involved no radical reorganization of the Army's logistical system. In *From Root to McNamara: Army Organization and Administration, 1900–1963* (Washington, D.C.: U.S. Army Center of Military History, Government Printing Office, 1975), James E. Hewes, Jr., attributes this fact to the lack of a need for full mobilization. Since the Army expanded only about 150 percent, rather than many times over as in the world wars, and since it was not necessary to build a mass army from a tiny base, the crisis did not reach the proportions that had precipitated reorganization in the earlier conflicts. Hewes, no admirer of the largely independent technical services that operated during the Korean War, surely would agree with Huston's "Korea and Logistics" that "in some ways the Army's service and supply organization still seemed to embrace too much red tape, to encourage too much duplication of effort, and to be too ponderous for speedy operation."[28] Undoubtedly because there was no logistical reorganization during the Korean War, there is no published scholarly appraisal of how the system operated in the United States from 1950 to 1953.

In the theater, logistic support for the Army in Korea fell to Rear Headquarters, Eighth Army, in Yokohama. These duties were in addition to those of area administration in Japan. After 25 August 1950, when this headquarters became the Japan Logistical Command, it was in effect a theater communications zone organization. As such, it processed supply requisitions from the Eighth Army in Korea, maintained theater stock records, and ordered supplies from the United States for direct shipment to Korea or for the restocking of depots in Japan. The operation of ports, depots, and other installations in Japan for logistic support also came under its jurisdiction. In addition, the command retained Eighth Army's responsibility for occupation duties in Japan.

Huston's "Korean Logistics" and the theater history, "Logistics in the Korean Operations," present the doctrinal problems in the establishment of the Japan Logistical Command. Army doctrine in mid-1950 provided for three types of logistical commands: type A, to provide army and communications zone support to a combat force not exceeding 30,000 men or a reinforced division; type B, to furnish communications zone support to a combat force of not more than 100,000 men; and type C, to provide communications zone support to a combat force of approximately 400,000 men. All of these commands were envisioned as permanent organizations under approved

---

[28]Huston, "Korea and Logistics," *Military Review*, February 1957, p. 27.

tables of organization, with balanced groupings of combined services for logistical support. The type C command, which the command in Japan was designated, was supposed to include between 75,000 and 150,000 men. In actuality, the Japan Logistical Command contained twice as many soldiers, had occupation duties not contemplated by the doctrine, and suffered a shortage of qualified technical personnel that forced it to rely heavily on Japanese labor. Consequently, Huston notes, it had to remain on a table of distribution and did not become a permanent organization.

As the theater history explains, this type of experience was typical: "Because no plan existed in June 1950 for combat operations in Korea, a logistical support system was developed piecemeal from emergency to emergency."[29] On 4 July 1950 the Far East Command established the Pusan Base Command at the southeastern Korean port to provide logistical support for United Nations forces. With its organization not yet firm and the situation very fluid, the new command drew service-type units from the 24th Infantry Division. Other personnel

were obtained from various sources, including convalescents discharged from hospitals. All personnel available were put to work unloading the early shipments, without the formality of an organization. The Pusan port was an excellent one, but the movement of two infantry divisions through it in the period of a few days produced a crush of men and material. Supplies and equipment were transported to Korea as fast as they could be outloaded from Japan. The unloading at Pusan, however, could proceed faster than material could be moved inland by rail and, consequently, troops often moved to the combat zone with only their personal weapons. Some weaknesses of the hastily organized Pusan Base Command soon became apparent. Shortages of manpower and materiel were aggravated by a lack of logistical training and shortages of certain specific skills among available personnel were quickly revealed.[30]

On 13 July 1950 the Far East Command reorganized the Pusan Base Command as the Pusan Logistical Command, a provisional unit. Although organized as a type B logistical command according to a table of organization and equipment, the Pusan Logistical Command was designated on 20 July a table of distribution unit. In discussing this situation, the theater history does not make explicit the reason for the decision not to make the new command a permanent organization. The unsettled personnel situation appears, however, to have been the deciding factor.

---

[29]"Logistics in the Korean Operations," vol. I, frame 1030.
[30]Ibid., frame 1032.

Considering the small size of the area in which it operated, the theater history observes, the Pusan Logistical Command bore heavy responsibilities. In addition to supporting a large number of U.S. troops, the command also had to support various other United Nations units, to deal with torrents of refugees, to house and supply prisoners of war, and to operate subsidiary ports. After the landing of the U.S. X Corps and the establishment of the 3d Logistical Command on the west coast at Inchon in mid-September 1950, the Pusan Logistical Command became responsible for the supervision of the new command.

Unable to handle all of these responsibilities, the Pusan Logistical Command gave way to a new organization, the 2d Logistical Command, on 19 September. Employing mostly personnel from its predecessor, the 2d Logistical Command was, like the Japan Logistical Command, a type C configuration organized under a table of distribution that was based on a table of organization and equipment. This arrangement provided more personnel spaces than had been authorized for the type B Pusan Logistical Command. The Far East Command considered making the 2d Logistical Command an advance section of the communications zone that the Japan Logistical Command represented. Other factors, reported by the theater history, weighed against such a decision: the distance—about 600 air miles—between Pusan and Yokohama; the Japan Logistical Command's already heavy responsibilities; and the proximity of the 2d Logistical Command to the Eighth Army. Therefore, the Far East Command left the 2d Logistical Command under the control of the Eighth Army so that it would continue to operate as an army service command, receiving, storing, and forwarding supplies for the Eighth Army. The 2d Logistical Command forwarded most of the Eighth Army's requisitions to the Japan Logistical Command, although the army retained direct control of the requisitioning of some items.

The 3d Logistical Command, a type B organization designed to control 35,000 to 60,000 men in support of 100,000 troops, actually contained 9,000 service troops and supported the X Corps, whose strength was 69,000. When in October the X Corps moved to the east coast of Korea, the 3d Logistical Command remained in the Inchon-Seoul area but was attached to the 2d Logistical Command. The Eighth Army took over operations on the west coast with 200,000 troops, for whose support the 3d Logistical Command became responsible. Operating on the east coast without an accompanying logistical command, the X Corps received support from the Eighth

Army through the 2d Logistical Command. These near-kaleidoscopic shifts can best be followed in the theater history.

Both the theater history and Huston's "Korean Logistics" comment on the effects on logistics of the division of command responsibility between the Eighth Army and the X Corps. From the landing at Inchon until late in December 1950, when it came under operational control of the Eighth Army, the X Corps operated independently. D. Clayton James' *The Years of MacArthur*, vol. 3, *Triumph and Disaster, 1945-1964* (Boston: Houghton Mifflin, 1985) reveals that General MacArthur insisted on this division of responsibility despite the opposition of Lt. Gen. Walton H. Walker, the Eighth Army commander, and many officers on MacArthur's own staff. The theater history describes liaison and exchange of information between the Eighth Army and the X Corps during this period as inadequate. Although the 2d Logistical Command had to support the amphibious move of the X Corps to the east coast in October, the logisticians received no advance warning of the requirements of the operation. The consequent sudden depletion of 2d Logistical Command stocks hampered Eighth Army operations. Huston states that X Corps officers suspected Eighth Army units of appropriating supplies that came through Pusan earmarked for the X Corps and that the X Corps frequently sent supply requisitions directly to the Japan Logistical Command, rather than through the 2d Logistical Command.

With the Eighth Army reeling from the onslaught of Chinese forces in December 1950, the 3d Logistical Command evacuated Inchon for Pusan, where the 2d Logistical Command absorbed most of its units. The 3d Logistical Command remained a subordinate element of the 2d Logistical Command for the next two years.

Inundated with evacuated supplies from North Korea and with supplies from Japan and the United States originally scheduled for unloading at northern ports, in addition to regular shipments, the 2d Logistical Command faltered. Not only did supply organization and procedures break down, declares the theater history, they never recovered.

Huston and the theater history concur in the opinion that the 2d Logistical Command was an appropriate application of logistical doctrine but suffered from a lack of flexibility in regard to personnel. As the theater history explains, "problems developed from the attempt to mold the command according to standard T/O&E's. The concept of a permanent command organization to control a fluctuating number of service units was believed sound, but the T/O&E's of the assigned or attached units were not designed to enable the units to accomplish many of the tasks they were required to perform. It was necessary to improvise, and units learned to perform missions that were different from those for which they were designed."[31] A need for large numbers of laborers, which Huston believes should have been anticipated, resulted in the employment of over 100,000 Koreans and swelled the command into an unexpectedly big organization.

Despite these flaws, there was no further major reorganization of the logistical establishment in Korea until the war was two years old. In July 1952 (effective 21 August) the Commander in Chief, Far East Command, General Clark, established the Korean Communications Zone (KCOMZ) to relieve the commander, Eighth Army, of responsibility for logistical and territorial operations and political relations with the government of the Republic of Korea. The boundary between the new rear command and the Eighth Army area ran roughly along the 37th Parallel. On 1 August the 2d Logistical Command became the operating agency for the new Korean Base Section, whose boundaries were coterminous with those of the communications zone. In mid-October the 2d Logistical Command was officially transferred from the Eighth Army to the Korean Communications Zone and in November was reduced to zero strength. With responsibilities for territorial administration, prisoners of war, and civil affairs assumed by the communications zone, the Korean Base Section could focus its energies solely on providing logistical support for the Eighth Army. The base section dealt directly with the Eighth Army, so that only essential administrative matters were to go through KCOMZ headquarters. Requisitions to the Japan Logistical Command could emanate only from the base section, but the section could not submit requisitions directly to the United States.

Both the theater history and Huston criticize the overlapping of the Korean Communications Zone and the Korean Base Section. With its single, coextensive section, the communications zone could not maintain a strict division between its own planning and policy-making functions and the operating functions of its subordinate. The fact that the communications zone actually had operating functions of its own, in the areas of territorial administration, prisoners of war, and civil affairs, helped to blur the lines of distinction. Even in some seemingly routine supply matters, the communications zone became

---

[31]Ibid., frame 1048.

involved because of perceived effects on policy. Duplication, Huston and the theater history agree, was the inevitable result.

Organizationally, the Far East Command patterned the Korean Communications Zone after a type C logistical command, a TOE organization of 75,000 to 150,000 men capable of supporting a combat force of approximately 400,000 men. Because of troop ceilings and shortages of personnel, however, the communications zone had only about 30,000 troops assigned and had to support 800,000 United Nations and Republic of Korea combat troops in addition to well over a hundred thousand prisoners of war and civilian internees. Only the employment of Korean civilians, Republic of Korea units, and KATUSA personnel enabled the communications zone to meet the demands of the situation, according to the theater history.

Closer to the front lines, the Eighth Army had its own problems of logistical organization. It was a hundred miles between the southern boundary of the army area and the supply installations at Pusan, and there was a dearth of intermediate depots. The road network was limited, and the rail system was vulnerable. With these limited lines and centers of communications, logistical units and supply bases were situated well forward of where they normally would have been. The enemy had the air capability to damage these targets, but he never employed it. As the theater history points out, the forward concentration of bases was dangerous nevertheless.

Toward the other end of the chain of command, at the theater level, an important change took place on 1 October 1952. General Matthew B. Ridgway, Commander in Chief, Far East Command, organized Headquarters, U.S. Army Forces, Far East, to begin a process of decentralization of his control over administration and operations. The new headquarters became the principal Army administrative headquarters in Japan and absorbed the Japan Logistical Command. Huston explains that U.S. Army Forces, Far East, with responsibility for logistical support of the Korean Base Section, thus functioned as the base section of a theater communications zone while at the same time playing the role of a theater communications zone headquarters and theater army forces headquarters. KCOMZ's position in this setup was equivalent to that of an advance section of a communications zone. Yet as a communications zone, the Korean Communications Zone enjoyed equal status with U.S. Army Forces, Far East, as a major subordinate command of the Far East Command. Huston finds that with close coordination, the communications zone and the army forces headquarters were able to overcome most of the difficulties inherent in their unusual relationship. On New Year's Day of 1953, General Ridgway regularized the situation to some extent in a reorganization that made clear KCOMZ's subordination to the army forces headquarters.

In a general critique of the logistical organization, the theater history scores the failure to follow doctrine sooner and more closely. The two-year lag between the outbreak of war and the establishment of a communications zone and a theater army headquarters "burdened the field army with complex responsibilities not directly related to the conduct of combat operations." On the other hand, commanders of the Japan Logistical Command, the 2d Logistical Command, and the Korean Communications Zone "were limited in their authority and in flexibility of organization within their commands."[32] Logistical commands and organizations should have been permanently organized at reduced strength before the war, the theater history advises, so that they could form the nucleus of wartime organizations.

A contradiction here is apparent. Logistical doctrine in June 1950 did call for the establishment of overall entities of control, but it also prized "flexibility in the application of . . . principles of communications zone organization and of control of operations. The commander adopts the type of organization which will best accomplish his mission."[33]

Requirements

Flexibility proved to be a necessity in the establishment of consumption rates and replacement factors, as logisticians tried to adjust to war in Korea. Huston's "Korean Logistics" observes that the Army by June 1950 had realized the need to modify the standards that had become part of logistical doctrine and regulations in World War II. Faulty figures in that war had resulted from failure to take into account equipment returned to depot stocks for reissue, from inadequate reports of materiel consumed, and from poor supply discipline on the part of troops. Modifications appeared in supply bulletins issued in 1951 and 1952, but they did not wholly suit the Korean situation. Salvage and repair of equipment, very difficult in the mountainous Korean peninsula with long lines of communications, could not equal the feats accomplished in the European Theater of Operations in 1944-45. (Huston states that the World War II ex-

---

[32]Ibid., frames 1020, 1086.
[33]FM 100-10, *Field Service Regulations: Administration,* Aug [*sic;* Sep] 49, quoted in ibid., frame 1086.

perience in Europe formed the basis for postwar doctrine, but he does not explain why Pacific experience was neglected. Presumably, this selectivity derived from the postwar expectation of a much greater likelihood of war in Europe.) Equipment losses in Korea consequently were greater for some items. World War II consumption factors for petroleum, oil, and lubricants also proved to be, in the words of the theater history, "grossly inadequate."[34] Moreover, the Army had to support South Korean troops and other U.S. services, whose rates of consumption differed from those of the Army. Finally, Army consumption and losses varied from operation to operation, adding yet another difficulty.

To its credit, the Army did not always delay action on requirements standards until its official publications on the subject appeared. Huston cites a June 1951 announcement by the Department of the Army that a year's operations in Korea had prompted the reduction of the replacement factor for medium tanks to 10 percent per month from the World War II figure of 14 percent. Huston points out further that approved replacement rates served as planning figures and as guides in screening requisitions, so that in 1952 the actual replacement rate for medium tanks was about 3 percent. The Army used the 10 percent figure as a ceiling beyond which commanders would find it difficult to go without a very good explanation. (Huston neglects to explain the low rate for medium tanks, leaving the reader to assume that it was a function of their restricted employment in difficult terrain and a weaker tank opposition than the Army had encountered on World War II European battlefields.)

If the Army made serious efforts to adjust requirements to the Korean situation, it was perhaps not blameless in the matter of supply discipline. The theater history comments disapprovingly that

the desire to live at war in accordance with American standards at home was evident throughout the operation in Korea. This attitude, while understandable, was costly to indulge. It manifested itself in the form of ice cream factories, snack bars, theaters, and PX's as well as in the excessive consumption of ammunition and supplies. Justified in Korea because it was not an all-out war where the sacrifices fell with comparative evenness on the entire population, such an attitude would create a dangerous drain on our resources in any global war.[35]

Veterans of the Korean War might find this observation unfair; veterans of the Vietnam War might find it strikingly familiar. For the

---

[34]"Logistics in the Korean Operations," vol. II, frame 150.
[35]Ibid., vol. I, frames 107-08. See also frame 1019.

historian, probably the most salient aspect of the comment is its confirmation of the global prism through which official observers viewed events in Korea.

Huston also finds a lack of supply discipline among U.S. troops. He suggests that their poor attitude toward conservation of equipment, which led to waste and artificially high requirements, is attributable to their perception of an inexhaustible supply. Here he faults the Army for oversupply. "Much of the clothing and equipment issued to combat troops," he maintains, "was excess to what really was needed."[36] He also notes the attempts of local commanders to get more equipment than their units actually required. The mutually reinforcing nature of these elements of supply indiscipline is obvious.

Distribution

In the early stages of the war, the United States of necessity adopted a system of automatic supply distribution. A changeable tactical situation, Huston notes, did not provide a firm basis for the preparation of requisitions. Initial efforts to supply the forces in Korea directly from the United States were unsatisfactory, since shipping time was so great. Japan thus became an island depot from which the Pusan Logistical Command drew automatic shipments. The paucity of that command's advance information on the arrival of troops and equipment, the theater history observes, reinforced the pressure for automatic supply. Logisticians at Pusan employed World War II factors to determine fifteen-day increments of supplies to be shipped from Japan.

Withdrawing from North Korea in December 1950, U.S. forces suffered severe losses of equipment that prompted logisticians in Washington to develop a new type of emergency shipment. By 2 December the 2d Infantry Division had lost sixty-three of seventy-two artillery pieces, most of its vehicles, nearly all of its signal and engineer equipment, and large quantities of small arms and individual equipment. Army G-4 in the Pentagon responded with PINK, the code designation for a shipment that took as its quantitative yardstick the table of organization and equipment of an infantry division. The object was to ship at once all the equipment required to outfit an entire division—something that had not been done before. Only liaison airplanes, general-purpose vehicles, ammunition, and certain items nonessential to combat were omitted. The G-4 gave technical

---

[36]Huston, "Korean Logistics," ch. X, p. 21.

service chiefs permission to draw from Mutual Defense Assistance Program reserves and from National Guard stocks if depot stocks could not provide all that was needed. On 9 December, a week after the program's inception, five of six ships carrying the equipment were en route to the Far East. Stowed in order of relative urgency and in a manner designed to permit its unloading with the ships' gear alone, the equipment could be taken, if necessary, directly to a small port in North Korea. As it happened, the PINK shipment was routed to Yokohama because the Japan Logistical Command had in the meantime mounted a more conventional emergency shipment to Korea. Still, Huston, who relates the PINK story, reports that the G-4 considered the speed with which the PINK movement was accomplished to be superior to anything done in World War II. More important, the experience served as the model for a standard operating procedure.

By the summer of 1951, the tactical situation and the knowledge that came with experience permitted Far East Command logisticians to modify the system of automatic supply. Under the new method, the 2d Logistical Command submitted to the Japan Logistical Command, sixty days before desired delivery, monthly requisitions for thirty-day increments of supply. In turn, the Japan Logistical Command forecasted requirements for the forces in Korea and presented requisitions to the San Francisco port of embarkation. The port could program shipping accordingly. One goal was to ship directly to Korea when feasible, Huston observes.

The attempt at directness of shipment had another motive besides speed. Cost, as the theater history points out, increased with the length of the pipeline. It was considerably more expensive to move supplies to Korea via Japan. But speed, Huston in effect reminds us, is often antithetical to frugality — thus considerably less cargo moved by air, an expensive mode of transport, from the United States to the Far East Command than moved by air within that command. Air transportation in the Korean War, Huston concludes, was much more important in the movement of selected critical items and of casualties than in terms of tonnage moved.

Because the Army would have to depend on ships to move supplies, the Korean War came at a potentially dangerous time. In March 1950 the Army had begun to turn over its ocean-going ships to the Navy's Military Sea Transportation Service, which was to handle all military ocean transportation as a unification measure. Interservice rivalry or simple confusion during this transition could have threatened the nation's ability to respond to the Korean crisis. Huston reports, however, that the move went smoothly and that it was completed in the Far East on 1 July, worldwide in November 1950.

A greater threat to military transportation proved to be the number of ships available for service. To meet the Army's greatly expanded needs, the Military Sea Transportation Service had to rely on chartering private U.S. vessels and breaking out ships from the "mothballed" Reserve Fleet. While waiting for the vessels from the Reserve Fleet to be made seaworthy, the service resorted to chartering foreign ships. Huston finds that shipping resources adequately met the requirements of the Korean War, with the possible exception of LSTs (landing ship, tank), which were much in demand in the Far East Command due to limited port facilities in Korea.

As with rebuild operations and procurement, Japan was extremely important for its extensive port resources. The Transportation Corps divided its port operations in Japan into three areas, with the largest centered at Yokohama on Tokyo Bay and lesser ones at Kobi (like Yokohama, on the main island, Honshu) and Moji (on the southern island, Kyushu). Boasting a fleet of 700 barges and the excellent dockyard facilities so necessary to keep essential port craft afloat, Yokohama handled roughly two-thirds of the sea traffic to and from Japan, according to Huston.

Supplies that arrived in Japan went into a depot system that Huston traces back to the beginning of the occupation of that nation by U.S. forces in 1945. By mid-1951 these depots were stocking approximately 800,000 different types of items (presumably many more than had been required for the occupation forces alone, although Huston does not say so). Such an array of supplies and equipment would have been hard enough to keep track of under the best of circumstances; war conditions made the task much more difficult. Supply paper work often did not keep up with changed destinations for the materiel. Rebuilt items sometimes were counted more than once on inventories. Judging from the evidence that Huston presents, supply accountability was not among the triumphs of the war. This appraisal must be considered in light of the crucial service that the depots in Japan performed, if a balanced view is to be obtained.

When programmed supply shipments began in July 1951, the Japan Logistical Command intended that 80 percent of the shipments by water from Japan to Korea eventually would be programmed. The logisticians in Japan also hoped that half of all future shipments to Korea would come directly from the continental United States. Within six months they had achieved the first goal, and by October 1952, 94 percent of all cargo shipped from Japan to Korea was programmed. They never quite attained the second objective; after reaching a high of 47 percent in May 1952, the percentage of shipments that went directly from the United States to Korea declined. Huston offers the same explanation as the U.S. Army Forces, Far East, which was that a backlog of lumber in Japan, combined with a decrease in the intensity of the war, kept this percentage down.

No matter its origin, most of the cargo that arrived in Korea went through the port of Pusan. The tactical situation, when bleakest, helped to ensure this fact. But the main reason for the preeminence of Pusan's small but excellent harbor was its deep-water dock facilities, which enabled it to handle a substantial volume of general cargo. Among other Korean ports, only Masan, about twenty miles west of Pusan, could provide deep-water berthing and then only for two ships. Besides berthing close to thirty deep-water vessels, Pusan could unload twelve to fifteen LSTs at once. All of this capacity translated into a daily discharge potential of 40,000 to 45,000 measurement tons, Huston reports, but problems of personnel and inland transporttion held the actual capacity to about 28,000 tons daily. (Huston also gives a figure of 14,000 tons for Pusan's actual average daily discharge rate in fiscal year 1951.)

Strategy and geography combined to make Inchon the second busiest port during the war. The site of X Corps' very successful landing in September 1950, Inchon lies only fifteen miles from Seoul, the capital of the Republic of Korea. As far as other natural amenities were concerned, the port had little to recommend it. Schnabel's *Policy and Direction* comments that "from the standpoint of navigation, sea approaches, and landing beaches, Inchon ranked among the worst harbor areas in Korea. The Yellow Sea in its periodic surges into the harbor (changes in the sluggish, heavy tide exceeded thirty feet) had created broad mudbanks and tidal flats which fronted the entire harbor. These flats were so soft and the muck so deep they would not support men on foot. Twice a day the tides rolled in to cover these flats."[37] A redeeming feature was a tidal basin built by the Japanese years before. The basin could accommodate nine small vessels, but most deep-water ships had to be unloaded by ship-to-shore lighters. Inchon's initial daily handling capacity, according to Huston, was only about 5,000 measurement tons, although this figure later increased somewhat. Other Korean ports did not even approach Inchon's capacity; their usefulness was confined to local operations.

---

[37]Schnabel, *Policy and Direction,* p. 146.

All of the Korean ports presented in common several problems of operation for the Army. The lighters and other harbor craft required at Inchon and elsewhere were not readily available in Korea and had to be brought from Japan. There were few experienced stevedores. Breakage and pilferage rates in the ports were high. Language difficulties were considerable. Huston observes that it was not easy for logisticians "to keep track of what had been unloaded . . . when Korean tallymen were found to be listing so many boxes of 'This Side Up,' and so many cartons of 'Handle with Care.'"[38] The stevedores successfully struck in the summer of 1952 for a daily wage increase to $1.40 from 50 cents. In special situations the Army arranged to have Japanese stevedores accompany cargo ships from Japan. For movements of the X Corps in November and December 1950, a Japanese-owned barracks ship carrying Japanese labor gangs enabled the corps to use a mobile work force in the ports. These laborers could do nothing, however, to alleviate the lack of transportation facilities for moving cargo out of the port areas, which Huston believes was probably the greatest limitation on port capacity in Korea. He criticizes the practice of establishing depots in the ports themselves as serving only to aggravate overloading. Turn-around time increased considerably as ships sat in port for three weeks waiting to be unloaded. Under such conditions, logistical organizations fell behind in making stock records, and many items could not be found when needed.

In general, Huston finds that "most of the transportation difficulties, once support activities had been stepped up after the initial impact of war, were to be found in Korea itself rather than in the long supply lines from the United States and Japan." He describes transportation in Korea as being "subject to severe limitations of geography. An almost uninterrupted chain of mountains extending from northern Korea all along the east coast and through the middle of the peninsula c[a]nalized communications through intervening valleys and corridors and along the relative lowlands of the west coast. Over 70 percent of the country had slopes greater than 30 percent." Climatic conditions were no better. "During the rainy season, between June and September, secondary roads often became impassable, and heavy flash floods imperiled fords and low-level bridges. Typhoons were likely to jeopardize air and sea transportation once or twice during late summer or early fall. Summer tended to be hot and humid, winters cold and dry."[39]

---

[38]Huston, "Korean Logistics," ch. XI, pp. 23-24.
[39]Ibid., ch. XII, pp. 1-3.

These topographic and climatic features alone would have provided a strenuous challenge to supply distribution, but the concentration of depots at Pusan made the problem even tougher. A year into the war, Huston notes, there were nine depots for various types of supplies in the Pusan area and only three depots elsewhere in the combat zone. Minimal further decentralization during the rest of the war did not essentially change this concentration.

Between the troops on the line and the depots at Pusan there were several types of supply installations. Closest to the divisions were supply points, about twenty-five to thirty miles behind the lines. "Some distance" (Huston's indefinite phrase) to the rear of each major supply point was a back-up point that, like the supply point, maintained a three- to five-day stock of supplies. The back-up point stood ready as a supply point in reserve. "Still farther to the rear" (again Huston's phrase) were regulating points that acted as valves to control the flow of materiel to the forward points.[40] Under standard operating procedure, the regulating points kept two days of supplies on rail cars that could be moved forward as needed. Movement from the supply points to division dumps ordinarily was by division-controlled rail or truck. Regiments then employed their own transportation to get the supplies to regimental dumps.

"In Korea," Huston declares, "the logistical effort depended above all upon the successful operation of the railroads."[41] On any given day in 1951, he reports, there were likely to be more than thirty trains dispatched, about three-quarters of them carrying supplies to forward railheads. These trains, composed of twenty to forty cars each, transported approximately 500 tons of freight an average distance of 100 miles. The Military Railway Service, controlled by the Transportation Corps and run by local employees of the Korean National Railway, was an offshoot of the organization with the same name that served the occupation troops in Japan. Dogged by a persistent shortage of freight cars, in mid-1951 the service had to cope with about one-third of its cars idled, waiting for unloading at or near the railheads. It was not unusual for cars to sit loaded for weeks. As the theater history points out, the establishment of intermediate depots between Pusan and the frontline areas would have alleviated this situation by providing greater storage space. Huston identifies other elements—a shortage of trained service troops, a lack of handling equipment, and lax control—that contributed to bottlenecks.

---

[40]Ibid., ch. VII, pp. 47–48.
[41]Ibid., ch. XII, p. 10.

Rail transportation was essential because truck movement of supplies could not replace it. Outside of the Inchon-Seoul highway and a few other radial roads from the Seoul hub, Korean roads were very poor. Substantial improvements of road surfaces and bridges by American engineers helped but by no means solved the problem. Moreover, the Army did not have enough trucks in Korea to take over the transportation load in the event of a major failure of the rail system. Huston observes that the number of transportation truck units assigned to support the Eighth Army was significantly less than the calculations based on World War II experience. More trucks would have cost more money, in terms of fuel and maintenance; rail transportation was more economical. But Huston seems to believe that the usefulness of trucks in the final stage of the distribution system, in getting the supplies from the railheads to the divisions, should have outweighed considerations of economy. He also wonders how the Army would have coped with a serious disruption of the rail system by enemy action, if there were not enough trucks to take up the burden.

Trucks formed an important part of an "informal distribution system," as Huston calls it, that developed because of the lack of intermediate depots. Huston likens the long supply lines to "long-range electrical transmission lines over which electrical energy loses its force unless booster stations make up some of the loss. In this case the 'booster stations,' i.e., intermediate depots, were missing. . . . The long distance of the depots from the combat divisions seemed to dull the sense of urgency in men operating the depots. Some of the divisions found it useful to station 'expediters' near the depots to see that badly needed supplies moved forward."[42] Truck convoys sometimes were the means of getting the supplies to the divisions. Such convoys operated outside the regular distribution system and depended on personal contacts between noncommissioned officers in division supply elements and their counterparts at the Pusan depots. Huston cautions that no matter the short-range success of such expedients, over the long term they could stimulate hoarding and thereby create artificial shortages.

The great distance between the Pusan complex and the front reinforced an existing tendency to locate supply points farther to the rear than was convenient for the divisions being supplied. The farther the depot was to the rear, the closer to Pusan and therefore the easier the

---

[42]Ibid., ch. VII, pp. 50-51.

trip between the depots and the supply points. This disposition went hand in hand with a "once burned, twice cautious" attitude stemming from having forward supply points overrun by the enemy during the war's volatile first year. In addition, deficiencies in roads, transportation, and personnel combined to make the supply points rather immobile. Huston concludes that this immobility contributed to the supply points' vulnerability and that the location of the supply points consequently was justified. By implication, the need for safety overbalanced the convenience of the divisions being supplied.

But there remains the question of why the Army did not establish a system of intermediate depots. Huston finds that for the 2d Logistical Command it was a question of personnel. The responsible officers realized the nature of the problem but lacked the numbers of service troops required to man intermediate depots.

Manpower ultimately proved to be the key to the last and most difficult segment of the pipeline from Pusan to the front lines. Beyond the supply points, the trucks carrying supplies negotiated rocky mountain roads as far as they could. When the roads petered out, the Army had to rely on Korean hand carriers. Originally recruited on an ad hoc basis, these carriers were not always reliable. The Army therefore arranged to have them organized into the Civil Transport Corps under the immediate supervision of ROK Army officers and the control of the Eighth Army transportation officer. Using an A-frame, each carrier was expected to transport fifty pounds of supplies ten miles daily. Performance improved under the new organization, but the workers still lacked military discipline and training. In mid-1951 the Army replaced the civilian organization with the Korean Service Corps, a military entity formed partially from ROK Army units. The new corps absorbed the old one and several other labor groups. Carriers now had military training and labored under full military discipline. Huston judges the Korean Service Corps to have been a much more dependable organization than its predecessor. The theater history, less enthusiastic, grants only that the Korean Service Corps "was considered more efficient."[43]

Huston considers alternatives to the hand carriers and finds them inadequate because of either insufficient availability or prohibitive cost. Cargo helicopters were very useful, but few of them were available before 1953. The Army employed airdrops, mostly from planes based in Japan, since Korea had a paucity of airfields and air

---

[43]"Logistics in the Korean Operations," vol. I, frame 1135.

base facilities. This method was very costly. Pack animals probably would have served well in the circumstances, but their importation to Korea, which lacked suitable mules and donkeys, would have involved expense greater than the Army was prepared to bear.

Logistics and Operations

Ports, railways, roads, and hand carriers—these and the other facets of the distribution system were all means to achieve the objectives of operations. Between logistics and operations there was—and is—a reciprocal relationship in which each affected the other. This relationship, implict in the above discussion of distribution, centered in the Korean War around problems of organization, coordination and planning, physical difficulties, and enemy action.

Enemy action was the cause of the retreat of the 25th Infantry Division from the central front to Masan during the first week of August 1950. The movement of the 25th Division, which had arrived in Korea between 10 and 15 July, was part of a withdrawal to the Pusan Perimeter, a rectangular area extending north from Pusan. Appleman's *South to the Naktong* describes some of the logistical trials that the division encountered in its 150-mile move, completed within thirty-six hours. A single road was available for about half the journey; at the halfway point the division was able to pick up a rail line. Since the road was the main supply artery to the central front, Eighth Army headquarters allotted all the officers it could spare to alleviate confusion as the troops moved south and supplies moved north. At the railhead, there was a great demand for rail equipment to evacuate supplies and troops.

Congestion in rail yards was almost indescribable. Units seeking transportation commandeered locomotives, cars jammed the tracks, native refugees crowded into cars, and general chaos threatened. The ROK 17th Regiment, moving southwest at this time . . . further complicated the traffic problem. Without the planning, supervision, and hard work of American transportation troops, the Korean rail system would have failed at this time.[44]

Historians sometimes neglect to spell out the relationship between logistics and operations in this manner. Less than two weeks after the X Corps' landing at Inchon, General MacArthur advised the X Corps commander that the latter's staff officers had been making requests for supplies through the G-4 staff section of General Headquarters, Far East Command. This procedure was inappropriate, since the X Corps was supposed to send its supply requests through channels to

---

[44]Appleman, *South to the Naktong*, p. 249.

the Japan Logistical Command; furthermore, the procedure had resulted in delaying the arrival at the X Corps of urgently required items. Apparently this incident, related in the theater history, has been overlooked by later writers. Even the theater history does not link the breach of procedure to X Corps operations, probably because those operations were eminently successful until the Chinese intervention. But the question remains, if the supplies were urgently needed, how did their absence or the tardiness of their delivery affect operations? Similarly, Schnabel's *Policy and Direction* reveals decisions taken in September and October to reduce supply shipments to Korea in view of the bright tactical outlook but does not make clear what actions were actually taken and with what eventual result.

In general, however, the causes and consequences of logistical difficulties in October 1950 are treated more fully in the literature. Appleman's *South to the Naktong* states flatly that "the Eighth Army advance into North Korea had begun under great logistical difficulties and was supported only on the narrowest margin."[45] Short of supplies, the Eighth Army had to leave one of its two corps behind when it advanced across the 38th Parallel. Appleman attributes this situation largely to the Eighth Army's inability to get supplies through the port of Inchon during the first half of October. The 1st Marine Division, outloading for operations on the east coast, tied up Inchon during that period — and in the process provided a clear demonstration of the value of port facilities to operations. Appleman also emphasizes the importance of the reconstruction of railroad and highway bridges for Eighth Army's progress. Despite prodigious engineering feats, on any given day in October the Eighth Army's I Corps front was roughly 200 miles beyond the railhead. "At every turn in the operations in North Korea" during the month, Appleman concludes, "Eighth Army's effort was limited by an adverse logistical situation."[46]

This situation continued past the middle of November. Appleman cites the Eighth Army's estimated daily requirement of 4,000 tons of supplies for offensive combat operations and notes that this level of support was not achieved until about 20 November. Until then, the theater history states, Eighth Army units operated with 3 to 4 days of rations. 1½ days of petroleum, oil. and lubricants, and 1 day of ammunition on hand. Consequently, General MacArthur had to delay until 24 November a planned concerted attack by the Eighth Army and the X Corps north to the Chinese border. Both the theater

---

[45]Ibid., p. 638.
[46]Ibid., p. 640.

history and Appleman convey MacArthur's emphasis on logistical difficulties as the cause of the delay.

As noted above in the section on "Logistical Organization," the X Corps in the fall of 1950 received its logistical support from the 2d Logistical Command of the Eighth Army, causing difficulty for both the X Corps and the Eighth Army. The suddenness with which the 2d Logistical Command had to shoulder the burden, the command's inadequate size for the task, and poor Eighth Army–X Corps coordination contributed to lateness in preparations for the concerted attack north. An example offered by the theater history involved a high-priority requisition received in October by the quartermaster, 2d Logistical Command, from the X Corps for winter clothing to outfit 40,000 X Corps troops. The X Corps did not notify the quartermaster, Eighth Army, of the requisition, but ordered the quartermaster depot at Pusan to fill the order. Although the depot did so, the resultant depletion of winter clothing stocks at Pusan delayed issues to the Eighth Army. Subsequently, the Eighth Army edited downward X Corps requisitions for various types of supplies, without informing the X Corps. The Eighth Army was confining the X Corps to the same level of supply as its own I and IX Corps, even though General MacArthur had approved a higher level for the X Corps. (It is not clear from the theater history's account whether the Eighth Army was aware of the dispensation.) In another case cited by the theater history, the 2d Logistical Command allowed the X Corps to receive supply ship cargoes whose contents the command had not checked, with the result that the corps got unbalanced lots. By late November, the X Corps had secured from General MacArthur authority to requisition all of its supplies directly from the Japan Logistical Command.

All of these logistical difficulties in the period after the Inchon invasion paled in comparison with those that the massive Chinese intervention of late November and December suddenly brought down upon the heads of U.S. Army commanders and logisticians. "Hardly could a more radical change have struck the supply system," Huston declares, "than that which came about in November and December 1950 when the distribution process had to be put into reverse. Almost overnight a situation in which pursuing combat divisions were outrunning their supplies, and service units were straining to catch up, changed to one in which pursued divisions streamed to the rear while service units strained to get out supplies before the enemy could overrun them."[47]

---

[47]Huston, "Korean Logistics," ch. VII, p. 55.

In the rapid movement north from the Inchon-Seoul area in October and November, the 3d Logistical Command had established an advance headquarters at the North Korean capital of Pyongyang, about 125 air miles north of Seoul. The Eighth Army also had set up supply points about forty to fifty miles north of Pyongyang. Retreating under the Chinese onslaught, Eighth Army elements closed these points and evacuated what supplies they could to Pyongyang. Swollen with this materiel in addition to what was already there, the city could not be cleared easily of all supplies before the arrival of enemy troops. As American troops fled south in what Huston describes as "near panic," the Eighth Army in the first week of December abandoned 8,000 to 10,000 tons of supplies in Pyongyang and destroyed another 2,000 tons that could not be saved in the nearby port of Chinnampo.[48] Mossman's "Ebb and Flow" is less harsh in appraising the conduct of the withdrawing troops, but reports the belief of the Eighth Army G-4 that a slower withdrawal from Pyongyang would have permitted the removal of most of the equipment there.

Materiel evacuated by sea from Chinnampo went to Inchon and Pusan, while most of that removed from Pyongyang was shipped overland to depots around Seoul and at Kaesong, about forty miles north of the capital. Mossman describes a system by which the remainder of supplies from Pyongyang was kept in the forward areas on rail cars that served as mobile supply points for the troops as they moved southward.

On the other side of the peninsula, the X Corps received orders on 8 December to evacuate its troops and equipment by sea from the port city of Hungnam and to move to the Pusan area. The Republic of Korea I Corps and large numbers of Korean civilians also were to be removed in the same operation. Schnabel's *Policy and Direction* points out that "there were no manuals to rely on in the planning and carrying out of the evacuation of such great numbers of troops and such great quantities of equipment from an area under constant enemy pressure. There was no time, either, for research or experimentation. Unlike Dunkerque, the evacuation plan called for the removal of all equipment and supplies."[49] The plan mandated the destruction, however, of any supplies that could not be loaded out in time.

Once the 1st Marine Division, an element of the X Corps, had been outloaded, the evacuation of materiel began in earnest on 15

---

[48]Ibid., pp. 55-56.
[49]Schnabel, *Policy and Direction*, pp. 301-02.

December. Mossman relates how "service units gradually moved depots and supply points into the port area proper, and the bulk supplies and heavy equipment were either loaded aboard ships double-banked at the docks or lightered to ships in the harbor. To save time, ammunition was loaded at the docks instead of well out into open water as is the more usual precautionary practice. This constant outward flow of materiel paralleled unit embarkations through the final day of the evacuation."[50]

Chinese efforts to disrupt the evacuation were confined to light, scattered thrusts, and by 24 December the outloading was complete. The X Corps reported that it had abandoned no serviceable equipment or supplies. Mossman states that about 200 tons each of ammunition and frozen dynamite, 500 thousand-pound aerial bombs, and about 200 drums of oil and gasoline were left behind, but that this materiel was destroyed. Schnabel tallies the people and materiel removed from Hungnam: 105,000 fighting men, 98,000 Korean civilians, 17,500 vehicles, and 350,000 tons of bulk cargo, comprising all together 193 shiploads.

"In retrospect," Mossman observes,

the evacuation of the X Corps from Hungnam had proved most spectacular as a logistical exercise. While the move could be considered a withdrawal from a hostile shore, neither Chinese nor North Korean forces had made any serious attempts to disrupt the operation or even to test the shrinking perimeter that protected the outloading. Logistical rather than tactical matters therefore had governed the rate of the evacuation. Indeed, the X Corps' redeployment south had been a matter of how rapidly . . . ships could be loaded.[51]

But the ultimate cause of the movement was, of course, the tactical situation. It was operational considerations that dictated a logistical undertaking for which there were "no manuals" or exact precedent.

The retreat of the Eighth Army on the west coast continued meanwhile, and in the first week of the new year, the army evacuated the port of Inchon and the nearby depot area of Ascom City. After the withdrawal from Pyongyang, the army had gradually reduced stocks at Inchon. Mossman points out that this forethought simplified the closing of the port. As his account indicates, and Huston's states, an increase in the orderliness of the move south below Pyongyang helped to make the removal from Inchon easier. Still, Mossman reveals, the Eighth Army commander, General Ridgway, found it

---

[50]Mossman, "Ebb and Flow," ch. X, p. 33.
[51]Ibid., pp. 40–41.

necessary to counter "the prevalent lack of spirit within his command" by specifically directing that no usable equipment be abandoned in the army's move south from Seoul.[52] Even with advance preparations, unforeseen staff delays, inadequate shipping, and overestimation in planned issues of ammunition to line troops forced the demolition of some moveable materiel at Inchon. Army engineers destroyed all main facilities, including the lock gates of the tidal basin, before leaving the port.

Huston describes how supplies that had been withdrawn gradually from the Inchon-Seoul area in December were redistributed to a series of new supply points ranging southeastward from near Seoul to within about fifty miles of Pusan. Each of these points, with a three-day stock of rations, gasoline, and ammunition, was to supply the withdrawing troops as they passed. This plan would obviate the need to move supplies constantly to the rear. A slower retreat than anticipated necessitated the resupplying of the initial point, but in general the system seemed to work well as the Eighth Army fell back past the second point and toward the third one in mid-January.

Late in January, General Ridgway began a cautious offensive that led the Eighth Army back to Seoul by mid-March and to the 38th Parallel by the end of that month. After a series of attacks and counterattacks over the next two-and-a-half months, the battle line stabilized a short distance above the 38th Parallel. Huston compliments the Eighth Army logistical units for their performance during this period. In withdrawals they evacuated supplies from forward supply points to predetermined back-up and regulating points without abandoning anything.

For the next two years, the war settled down to a still deadly but static affair without the dramatic operational and logistical shifts that had marked its first twelve months. The theater history's short chronological account of logistics from mid-1951 to the end of the war emphasizes a greatly increased need for engineer equipment in 1951 as both sides dug in. Despite continuing concerns about the supply of ammunition, supply for the most part became routine in 1952 and 1953 — perhaps too routine, in the view of General Maxwell G. Taylor, who had assumed command of the Eighth Army in February 1953. The theater history quotes General Taylor's warning that although the Eighth Army "achieved a tactical mobility which allowed it to shift its reserves readily to meet threatened points along the im-

---

[52]Ibid., ch. XII, p. 20.

mediate front, it depended for its mobility upon an elaborate supply system which would have been most difficult to displace if our forces had been required to move rapidly forward over considerable distances into enemy territory."[53] Taylor went on to criticize a system that had to depend on a railroad net working to capacity constantly, indigenous employees who could not advance with the army if necessary, and heavy impediments of post-type property accumulated during the stalemate. Perhaps the Eighth Army was fortunate that it did not have to test its commander's pessimistic vision.

Primary Sources

Industrial Mobilization

Essential for the study of pre-Korean War industrial mobilization planning and of military aspects of the actual mobilization of industry are the Records of the Munitions Board in the Records of the Office of the Secretary of Defense, Record Group (RG) 330, National Archives and Records Administration (NARA), at the Washington National Records Center (WNRC) in Suitland, Maryland. In addition to planning the military facets of industrial mobilization, the board was charged with evaluating the logistic feasibility of strategic plans, determining priorities within military procurement programs, and developing policy for military versus civilian requirements. The board's records, nearly all of which remain security classified, have been virtually unused by scholars. Arranged by organizational unit, and thereunder by functional series, the records run to over 1,000 linear feet. They include the files of the successive chairmen, the historian and special assistant to the chairman, and functional units dealing with requirements, programming, production, priorities, and controls, in addition to general records consisting mainly of minutes, reports, and correspondence. An unpublished finding aid provides, for each series, inclusive archival box numbers and a brief indication of the contents of each box. In the general records, the board's minutes are indexed, and the correspondence is filed under a decimal system. Thorough research on a given subject—tank requirements, for example—requires sifting not only through files of the apposite functional unit—in this case, the Office of the Vice Chairman for Production and Requirements—but also through the office files of each of the successive chairmen and, in the general records, the minutes, reports, and correspondence.

---

[53]"Logistics in the Korean Operations," vol. I, frame 1007.

A worker welds an M–46
tank turret while its 90-mm.
gun stretches menacingly
toward the arsenal skylight.

Motor equipment of the 25th Infantry Division waiting to be moved
aboard an LST at Sasebo Base, Kyushu, Japan, for shipment to the
battlefront in Korea.

U.S. Army ordnance troops
repair precision instruments
in a mobile tool shop near
the fighting front.

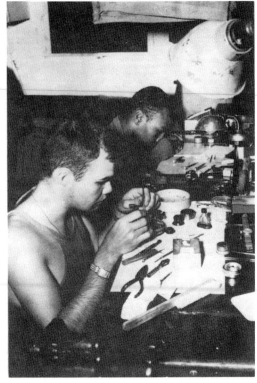

Port facilities with stockpiles of military supplies along the docks in the
port of Pusan, 9 August 1950.

A U.S. soldier sorts dirty uniform pants and jackets before they are taken to the quartermaster cleaners near Chunchon, about ten miles south of the 38th Parallel.

View of the harbor and city of Pusan, from a hill northwest of the center of the city.

LSTs and LCMs stranded by the low tide in the Yellow Beach area of Inchon, 19 September 1950.

Large piles of supplies on the docks at Inchon await truck transportation to the U.S. Eighth Army.

Cargo is loaded from the SS *Carleton Victory* to a DUKW in Inchon Harbor.

The U.S. X Corps Class I (principally food) dump at a supply point operated by men of the 545th Quartermaster Company, U.S. Eighth Army.

Drums of mobile gas at a reserve point.

A steam locomotive, part of equipment for United Nations troops, is hoisted from ship to dock at Pusan.

South Korean laborers and U.S. soldiers carry ammunition and food to frontline troops of the 1st Cavalry Division in the Waegwan area, about seventy miles northwest of Pusan.

The 187th Regimental Combat Team, cut off and stranded for forty-eight hours, receives supplies from the air in the midst of the conflict.

Troops of the 3d Logistical Command aboard an LST prepare to embark on an evacuation ship waiting in Inchon Bay, 22 December 1950.

The records of the Munitions Board's bureaucratic rival, the National Security Resources Board, are contained in the Records of the Office of Civil and Defense Mobilization, RG 304, NARA, in Washington, D.C. The Office of Civil and Defense Mobilization was a 1958 creation that absorbed the Office of Defense Mobilization (ODM), which in turn in 1953 had absorbed the National Security Resources Board and the older Office of Defense Mobilization that dated from 1950. Numbering about 430 linear feet, and mostly declassified, the NSRB records are divided into three main aggregations: records of the Office of the Chairman; records of the Administrative and Coordinating Staff; and records of the Mobilization Planning Staff, which are subdivided into two parts covering the periods 1947–51 and 1951–53, respectively. In general, within each of these major divisions there are two main types of series: central correspondence files and the files of individual officials. Arrangement within series varies, most being arranged either chronologically or alphabetically by subject. For three security-classified series, including NSRB general correspondence and reports, there is an alphanumeric filing system, the headings and subjects for which are listed in an appendix to a processed finding aid that describes all NSRB records briefly, down to the series level.

As with the Munitions Board records, subject area research in NSRB records involves the exploration of a variety of files. For the purposes being discussed here, the researcher would be most interested in the period 1947-50, when the National Security Resources Board had a significant planning responsibility, and from June to December 1950, when the agency held an important coordinating function. It can easily be seen from the above description of arrangement that for any topic, several series within each of the main divisions of the record group would have to be consulted.

Also part of RG 304 are the Records of the Office of Defense Mobilization and the Defense Production Administration (DPA). The National Archives is preparing a draft inventory of the entire record group, but at present there is no finding aid for the ODM and DPA records comparable to that for the records of the National Security Resources Board. Arrangement of the ODM and DPA records appears to be generally the same as that of the NSRB files—broad organizational groupings containing a series of correspondence files and the files of individuals. Established as a small organization concerned with policy guidance and control and with settling interagency differences, the Office of Defense Mobilization divided its mobilization activities into six major areas: stabilization, production, manpower, transportation, foreign supplies and requirements, and scientific research. The agency's files, which total about 140 linear feet, provide an overview of issues involved in wartime production and the division of manpower between the military and industry. Under the direction of the director of defense mobilization, the administrator of defense production heading the Defense Production Administration exercised general control of the defense production progam. Functionally organized, the administration contained four principal offices: Program and Requirements, Resources Expansion, Staff Service, and Procurement and Production. The administration sought to match supply against demand, certified appropriate financial aid to defense industries, and formulated basic policies and procedures for procurement and for achievement of production programs. Using this agency's approximately 110 linear feet of records, the researcher can trace the development of, and can appraise, policies designed to make the procurement programs of the military services operate as efficiently and economically as possible.

A small amount of DPA planning and programming records is contained in the Records of the National Production Authority (NPA), RG 277, NARA, in Washington, D.C. Created by President Truman in September 1950 as an element of the Department of Commerce, the National Production Authority was responsible for developing and promoting production and supply of defense materials and facilities, for determining that the needs of the civilian economy were adequately represented in the defense effort, for ensuring the equitable distribution of critical materials after defense needs were met, and for ensuring that small businesses were participating in defense contracts. There is no adequate finding aid for the 564 linear feet of NPA records, but a perusal of a series of sixty-two historical reports (one of the original sixty-three is missing) prepared by the agency indicates that its primary focus was on the allocation of critical materials for civilian production once military production had been satisfied. Perhaps of most value to the researcher focusing on the concerns of the present study are the files of the agency's various commodity bureaus (such as Metals and Minerals, Chemical, Rubber, and Forest Products), which provide a view of an initial link in the chain of military production, and the files of the Office of Civilian Requirements, which acted as spokesman for civilian needs. If a full mobilization had developed during the Korean War, the NPA records would be of much greater importance, since the competition between the military and civilian sectors for materials would have been much more intense.

The researcher should not overlook the Records of the Industrial College of the Armed Forces in the Records of Interservice Agencies, RG 334, NARA, in Washington, D.C. These records include lectures by participants—often prominent—in mobilization, sometimes containing candid comments of a type not easily found elsewhere. Bound copies of the lectures are also available at the National Defense University Library at Fort Leslie J. McNair in Washington, D.C.

Defense Department policy and efforts in industrial mobilization can be explored in the secretary's files in the Records of the Office of the Secretary of Defense, RG 330, and in the Records of the United States Joint Chiefs of Staff, RG 218, both held by NARA in Washington, D.C. (For a discussion of the arrangement of these records, see the next section below.) In both record groups, documents on industrial mobilization can be found under decimal classification 004.04.

Collections of the personal papers of several industrial mobilization figures are available. At the Harry S. Truman Library in Independence, Missouri, are the papers of Donald F. Carpenter, Munitions Board chairman, 1948–49, and Jarold A. Kieffer, assistant in the Office of Defense Mobilization, 1951–58. The papers of Lt. Gen. LeRoy Lutes, staff director of the Munitions Board, 1948–49, are in the National Archives Gift Collection, RG 200, NARA, in Washington, D.C.

Manpower Mobilization and Logistics—the Continental United States

In the Records of the Office of the Secretary of Defense, RG 330, almost all of the main policy file through the Korean War period, originally security classified, has been declassified. The arrangement of this material up to July 1950 is by a numerical filing system, the key to which is not available with the records. Beginning with July 1950, the records are arranged by the old War Department decimal file system. For the main policy file there is an index, alphabetical by subject, in the Records of the Office of the Administrative Secretary, Correspondence Control Section. Under "Korea" can be found a chronological listing of documents with a notation of the sender or recipient and subject of each. Considerable material on manpower mobilization and materiel issues resides in file CD 092 Korea. These records are useful, particularly in regard to manpower levels and worldwide allocation of forces, in establishing the context for policy making at the cabinet level.

Also in RG 330 are the Records of Anna Rosenberg, Assistant Secretary of Defense (Manpower and Personnel), Relating to Manpower and Personnel Matters of the Department of Defense. Declassified and arranged by War Department decimal, these four linear feet of records include information on perceived inequities in reserve recalls, the release of involuntarily recalled reservists, and Army strength ceilings. Other, smaller, series in the records of the assistant secretary's office are also helpful in regard to manpower plans, policies, and procedures.

The Records of the United States Joint Chiefs of Staff (JCS), RG 218, are a valuable resource because of the JCS system of staff actions, in which the service staffs study and comment upon proposals. Often the Army's position can be viewed in some detail in the JCS files. The main body of records is divided into two large series, the first arranged by War Department decimal and the second alphabetically by name of foreign country and thereunder by War Department decimal. In each series the arrangement within individual decimals is chronological and divided into "sections." At the beginning of each section there is a chronological list of all the documents in the section and in preceding sections under the same decimal.

Finding material filed by the War Department decimal system in RG 218 presents the same challenge that the researcher faces anywhere that system is employed: in the best Collingwoodian fashion, reenacting the thoughts of long-departed file clerks to determine under what subject decimals documents on a particular topic should be filed. Tutelage under experienced archivists and imaginative use of *War Department Decimal File System*, rev. ed. (Washington, D.C.: Government Printing Office, 1943), will enable the careful researcher to find most of the documents relevant to his work. In the main JCS decimal file, a great deal of material on manpower planning and mobilization can be found in decimals 370 and 381; 320.2 contains information on force strength. Records in the geographic file under the headings of "Far East" and "Korea" and thereunder in decimals 381 and 383.21 also provide much on the relation between manpower decisions and the situation on the ground. It is somewhat more difficult to extract information on logistics, and the researcher must resign himself to slogging through a variety of decimals in the 400 series, which deals with supplies, services, and equipment. Diligent searching will also reveal caches of information in other classifications. For example, decimal 320 covers organization of the Army, and a subdivision of that classification is 323, geographical divisions. Under a further subdivision, 323.3, military departments and divisions, will be found informative files on "Policy and Guidance in Logistics Matters on Port Operations."

Separate from the main JCS records, and much less voluminous, are the chairman's files. In the files of General of the Army Omar N. Bradley, chairman during the Korean War, under decimal 091 Korea, there is a small amount of material dealing with manpower issues such as replacements.

Moving down to the service level, the Records of the Office of the Secretary of the Army, RG 335, NARA, are at the WNRC, and the Records of the Office of the Chief of Staff in the Records of the Army Staff, RG 319, NARA, are in Washington, D.C. Most of RG 335, which is arranged by the War Department decimal system, is classified for the Korean War period. Almost all of the chief of staff's files, which are similarly arranged, are declassified for this period. Although the researcher occasionally may turn up in these two sources a useful document not to be found elsewhere, as a general rule the files of the assistant chiefs of staff will produce the great bulk of the relevant documentation on mobilization and logistics.

From the mobilization researcher's point of view, the Records of the Office of the Assistant Chief of Staff, G–3, in RG 319, NARA, in Washington, D.C., are primus inter pares. Staff actions dealing with mobilization centered in G–3, and its decimal files are rich in documentation for both the prewar and war periods. Some of the most valuable decimal classifications are: 091 (Korea), 110 (appropriations), 320 (organization), 320.2 (strength), 322 (activation of units), 325 (National Guard), 326 and 326.2 (Organized Reserve Corps), 327 and subordinate decimals (the draft and draftees), 353 (training), 370.01 (mobilization). Cross reference sheets at the beginning of each decimal classification greatly facilitate research. Much of the material dealing with the Korean War is declassified. The thorough researcher will wish to look also at the Records of the Office of the Assistant Chief of Staff, G–1, in RG 319, NARA, at the WNRC, most of which are declassified. An examination of the relevant decimal classifications in these records indicates, however, that most of the pertinent documents on manpower issues are duplicated in the G–3 files.

For logistical activities in the continental United States, the Records of the Office of the Assistant Chief of Staff, G–4, in RG 319, NARA, in Washington, D.C., are the principal source. Use of these records is more difficult than that of the G–3 files. Sparse research activity has meant few requests for declassification, and most of the G–4 records remain security classified. For the main decimal file there is a massive "index" consisting, for the Korean War period, of roughly 120,000 reference sheets arranged chronologically by year, but the arrangement within years is not clear. Each sheet provides a reference to an individual document, giving the document's decimal classification file number but in many cases no date. Without a key to the arrangement of the reference sheets within each year, the researcher will find this "index" virtually useless. The researcher must resort to methodical searching of decimal classifications, particularly within the 400 series. Some general information on issue of equipment for the Korean War can be found under 400.35 Korea, but this functional classification for "issues" must be supplemented heavily with exploration of decimals for individual types of equipment—for example, 472.2 for 105-mm. howitzers, or 422.3 for cold weather clothing. Decimal 325 contains significant material on the transfer of National Guard equipment to the Regular Army, but again the careful researcher will want to check the decimals for the particular types of equipment discussed. In summary, the G–4 decimal files are much oriented toward a commodity approach and therefore defy attempts to get a full picture through use solely of the functional decimals.

The records of another Army staff agency, the Office of the Executive for Reserve and ROTC Affairs, in RG 319, NARA, in Washington, D.C., may be mined for individual documents that do not appear in the G-3 files. Arranged by War Department decimal classification, the records are declassified through the Korean War period.

Also declassified and arranged by War Department decimal, the Records of the National Guard Bureau, RG 168, NARA, are at the WNRC. Again, these records can best serve as a supplement to the G-3 files. Perhaps one of the most useful decimals is 319.1, which contains reports on the status of National Guard equipment. The researcher will be disappointed to find, however, that some important decimal files, such as 370.01 (mobilization), are thin.

Information on the status and training of mobilized units may be found in the Records of the Office of the Chief of Army Field Forces (OCAFF) in the Records of Headquarters Army Ground Forces, RG 337, NARA, in Washington, D.C. At first glance the OCAFF records present a prodigious task for the researcher, since there are both large central decimal files and separate files for each of a variety of staff sections, with no detailed overall guide. A series of annual histories in RG 337 prepared by the OCAFF Historical Section, however, assuages this difficulty. The comprehensive histories offer accounts of every important aspect of training, and more, including alerting procedures, equipment and combat readiness of National Guard units, studies of required equipment for Korea, and the replacement system. In addition, the histories' footnotes serve as guides to relevant documents in the various OCAFF files. Some of the cited documents are included in the histories. Most of RG 337 remains security classified for the Korean War period.

More problematical are the records of units, which are contained in the Records of United States Army Commands, RG 338, NARA, in the WNRC. At any organizational level, the records of a specific unit will not be found in a single location within the record group. Retirement of unit records by the Army to the National Archives has been sporadic and piecemeal, so that rarely do all of a unit's records for a given period appear in a single accession; nor does NARA know in most cases whether all extant records of a particular unit have been retired. RG 338 officially begins with the year 1942 (although there are, in fact, earlier files for some units in the record group), and typically an accession will include material covering the early 1940s

through the mid-1950s. Arrangement within an accession is generally
by type of document, such as general orders, conference and meeting
papers, historical files, memorandums, circulars, bulletins, planning
files, and operations orders. The researcher thus must explore half-a-
dozen or more types of files within each accession for a specific unit.
A group of some of the accessions is covered in a series of index cards
that show the unit, the type of file, and inclusive dates for each type
of file. Since the cards provide carton numbers for each type of file,
the researcher can get an approximate idea of the amount of material
in each case. Documentary coverage varies rather widely from unit to
unit and drops off noticeably below the division level.

For information on the training of specific units, the researcher
may consult the records of the appropriate training centers in RG
338; but here also, the amount of material varies widely. The
WNRC's holdings are assembled for each installation in an aggrega-
tion covering the early 1940s to the early 1950s and may fill only one
box or as many as a thousand. Arrangement for the most part is by
functional unit within the installation and thereunder by type of
document (such as general orders, memorandums, and general correspondence). For each installation there is a finding aid that gives
minimal information as to number of boxes and types and date spans
of material. The bulk of the records deal with the pre–Korean War
period. Some installations are not represented by any documentation.
Almost all of the material is classified.

The researcher can supplement the official sources with the per-
sonal papers and oral histories of some of the participants. At the
U.S. Army Military History Institute, Carlisle Barracks, Penn-
sylvania, there are collections of the papers of General Matthew B.
Ridgway, deputy chief of staff for administration, 1950; Gordon
Gray, assistant secretary of the Army, 1947-49, and secretary of the
Army, 1950; and General Lewis B. Hershey, director of selective ser-
vice, 1941-73. Oral histories by Hershey and Lt. Gen. Milton
Reckord, an influential National Guard Association official, are also
available at the institute. In Independence, Missouri, the Harry S.
Truman Library has the papers of Lt. Gen. Thomas B. Larkin, Army
staff G-4, 1949-52, and an oral history interview with Gordon Gray.
The Dwight D. Eisenhower Library in Abilene, Kansas, holds
another collection of Gray's papers, in addition to those of General J.
Lawton Collins, Army chief of staff, 1949-53. At the Citadel in
Charleston, South Carolina, are the papers of General Mark W.
Clark, chief, Army Field Forces, 1949-52. Columbia University in
New York City possesses oral history interviews with Clark and Gray.

Published memoirs of participants are generally of minimal value to the historian of mobilization and logistics. Omar N. Bradley and Clay Blair's *A General's Life: An Autobiography* (New York: Simon and Schuster, 1983) deals extensively with major events and decisions in Washington but concentrates on their relation to strategy and operations with only occasional mentions of manpower and logistics. Relying heavily on official Army histories, J. Lawton Collins' *War in Peacetime: The History and Lessons of Korea* (Boston: Houghton Mifflin, 1969) gives sporadic attention to logistical problems but focuses on strategy, operations, and budgets. The same author's *Lightning Joe: An Autobiography* (Baton Rouge: Louisiana State University Press, 1979) contains only a summary of the principal events of the war, during which he was Army chief of staff. Mark W. Clark's *From the Danube to the Yalu* (New York: Harper & Brothers, 1954) and Maxwell D. Taylor's *Swords and Plowshares* (New York: W. W. Norton & Co., 1972) provide little of use on the authors' tours of duty as chief, Army Field Forces, and deputy chief of staff for operations, respectively. In *The Korean War* (Garden City, N.Y.: Doubleday & Co., 1967) and *Soldier: The Memoirs of Matthew B. Ridgway* (New York: Harper & Brothers, 1956), General Ridgway, who served as deputy chief of staff for administration in 1950, views the war mostly in terms of operations, strategy, and politics. *The Minute Man in Peace and War: A History of the National Guard* (Harrisburg, Pa.: Stackpole, 1964) must be considered a primary source for the Korean War period since its author, Maj. Gen. Jim Dan Hill, was chairman of the Army's General Staff Committee on National Guard and Reserve Policy in the early 1950s. He describes the guard's weaknesses in the years preceding the war and confidently offers the argument that the reserve components should have been completely mobilized at the beginning of the war to achieve a quick victory.

Manpower Mobilization and Logistics—the Far East Command

For the entire range of activities in the Far East Command, there is one indispensable group of sources: the command reports from the various echelons, assembled conveniently in the Records of The Adjutant General's Office, RG 407, NARA, at the WNRC. Here is a vast store of information that must form the core of any history of theater events.

Army regulations in force when the Korean War began required the preparation of an annual narrative historical report rather than a periodic command report. The Army began to require a wartime monthly command report in October 1950. For the period 1 January to 31 October 1950, the Far East Command prepared a single report in the annual format. This narrative contains an eighty-page overview of all facets of command activities, including operations, intelligence, personnel, logistics, and miscellaneous, in addition to a section on problems, solutions, and lessons learned. The report also includes a report from each of the command's staff sections with roughly a hundred supporting documents each for the G-1 and G-4 sections. Appended to the G-1 report is a very detailed (about two thousand pages) daily war diary containing a minute-by-minute log of messages, radios, memorandums, and other communications.

Since the Eighth Army was relieved from the requirement to submit an annual-format report for the period 25 June to 31 October 1950 (there is no historical report covering the unit from 1 January to 25 June), the historian must rely on the Eighth Army's war diaries for the crucial early months of the war. For reasons not immediately clear, there is no command report in RG 407 from the Eighth Army for November 1950, although there are war diaries. The diaries are detailed daily renderings of events, with feeder reports from Eighth Army staff sections. Because of the closeness of coverage in these diaries, trends can be determined only with a great amount of work collating and synthesizing these details. In each month of the diaries, Section I is a chronological summary of activities, while Section II includes the war diary itself along with daily staff section reports and supporting documents. Section I, which can run over a hundred pages, concentrates on operations; coverage of G-1 and G-4 activities is sketchy compared to the later command reports. The section can be used, however, as a guide to the detailed daily reports in Section II.

When instituted in October 1950, the command report requirement reached down to the battalion level and included nontactical commands. Since the format of the reports is roughly uniform at all levels of command, a description here of an Eighth Army report should suffice to convey the type of information that all the reports contain. The level of detail naturally increases as one moves down the chain of command.

For January 1951 the command report of the Eighth Army is divided into four parts: Section I, Table of Contents (useful in locating individual staff section reports quickly); Section II, Narrative, subdivided into Background, Plans and Preparations, Enemy Situation, and Operations; Section III, Staff Section Reports; and Section IV, Graphic Arts Supplement, including such items as maps and charts. In Section II, the subdivision on operations is in turn divided into Personnel, Tactical Operations, and Logistics. The narrative on personnel, in a few pages, provides the overall strength of the Eighth Army and briefly discusses casualties, both battle and nonbattle; gives the number of replacements received, both officer and enlisted; lists the expected daily average number of replacements in various career fields; discusses difficulties in transporting replacements from Pusan, and the establishment of small replacement detachments in various locations; and treats the prospective employment of KATUSA personnel. In about thirty-five pages, the narrative on logistics discusses the general logistical situation; gives a breakdown, by element (such as Eighth Army and KATUSA), of supported strength; provides statistical information on, and discusses problems and innovations in regard to distribution of, the various classes of supplies; treats local procurement, enemy materiel, salvage, post exchange rations, special services supplies, civil affairs supplies, prisoner of war supplies, evacuation of casualties, evacuation of prisoners of war, and evacuation of refugees; discusses methods employed, problems encountered, and tonnage moved in transportation by highway, rail, water, and air; and describes the effects of the loss of the port of Inchon on the replacement pipeline.

In Section III, Staff Section Reports, the assistant chief of staff, G–1, provides a four-page command report (by the G–1 historical officer) that covers strength and casualties; the general situation and problems in regard to replacements; prisoners of war; Korean personnel; morale and personal services; discipline, law, and order; and plans. Attached to the G–1 report are thirty-eight enclosures. Each of the first thirty-one enclosures covers a single day of January 1951 and includes a journal summary of one or two pages by the G–1 historical officer. The subjects dealt with in the journal summaries always include casualties but otherwise vary with events — replacements, law and order, visits, interior management, morale activities, and promotions appear frequently. Following the journal summary is the journal itself, which is a log, primarily of documents, with a one-line description of each document. Occasionally one or two selected documents are appended to the journal. Enclosures 32 through 35 to the G–1 report are graphs that give a weekly breakdown, by division and regimental combat team, on the strength of U.S. combat units, replacements, battle casualties, and nonbattle casualties. Enclosure 36 is a graph showing replacements and returns to duty in U.S. combat units from June 1950 through January 1951. Cold weather casualties, 29 December 1950 to 26 January 1951, are given in a graph at enclosure 37. Enclosure 38 deals with an officer reassignment study.

The body of the report of the assistant chief of staff, G-4, in Section III is very brief. In little more than a page, the report lists the principal logistical problems at the beginning of the period; describes the final evacuation of the Seoul-Inchon area, citing the major decisions and the amount of supplies destroyed; gives the major decisions and events of the subsequent "retrograde movement"; and sketchily describes the situation at the end of the period. There are thirty-one enclosures to the report, each consisting of a daily Eighth Army G-4 journal with annexes. Generally there are six annexes: Periodic Logistical Reports (statistics); Radios; Letters; Administrative Orders; G-4 Division Journals (one journal each for the divisions that composed the Eighth Army G-4 section); and G-4 Briefing Notes (statistics). With all the enclosures and annexes, the G-4 report runs to perhaps a thousand pages. Except for the quick overview that comprises its main body, the G-4 report is essentially raw data.

During the last two-and-a-half years of the war, changes in the format of the command reports were mostly minor. Generally, there was a modest but helpful increase in the length of the narrative sections. A major change came in May 1953 with the revision of the format of the body of the report into two sections: a narrative with analysis, and recommendations. At the end of the war, however, there was still considerable uncertainty as to how the section on recommendations was to be presented.

Command reports of General Headquarters, Far East Command, are contained in 528 archives boxes in RG 407. The Eighth Army command reports are in 418 boxes.

For the Japan Logistical Command in RG 407, there is an "Activities Report" for the period 25 August–30 September 1950. Monthly command reports begin in October 1950, but those for the early months of the war actually were not prepared until much later by the command's Historical Section. The reports are divided into three parts: narrative, enclosures (documents), and staff section reports. Averaging about 135 pages, the narratives contain sections on organization; personnel; operations and planning; logistics, subdivided into supply, evacuation and hospitalization, and transportation; and comment. The Japan Logistical Command reports fill approximately 240 archives boxes.

Much less voluminous are the reports of the Pusan Logistical Command and the 2d Logistical Command, which are contained together in four archives boxes. Among these documents are monthly activities reports for the period July to November 1950. These reports, arranged by staff section, are accompanied by the reports of the individual staff sections themselves. Selected documents are attached to the staff sections' reports. The command reports begin with December 1950 and include the main report, staff section reports, and the reports of engineer, military police, quartermaster, ordnance, transportation, and other units within the 2d Logistical Command. In the G–4 section reports there is a detailed "Log of Notes and Conversations" and a daily "Periodical Logistical Report."

The 3d Logistical Command submitted two "Historical Reports," one for October–November 1950 and one for November 1950, both of which include a narrative, staff section reports, and supporting documents. There is a single command report, for December 1950, with the same basic format as the historical reports. Since the 2d Logistical Command absorbed the 3d Logistical Command late in 1950, the latter stopped issuing command reports. The 3d Logistical Command's few reports are contained in four archives boxes.

Command reports of the Korean Base Section begin with July 1952 and end with April 1953 (the main section of the report for July 1952 is missing from RG 407). The reports, which are arranged basically the same as those of the other logistical units, reside in twenty-two archives boxes labeled "KCOMZ, KBS"; a search did not turn up any separate command reports for the Korean Communications Zone.

There are thirty-four boxes of command reports, covering October 1952 to July 1953, for Headquarters, U.S. Army Forces, Far East. These reports follow the expected general format.

A sampling of the Far East Command reports in RG 407 revealed that some are missing. Since the Historical Section of the command's headquarters collected copies of the reports and supporting material for the period 1950–52, it may be possible to fill some of the gaps from that section's records in the Records of Headquarters, Far East Command, which are in the Records of United States Army Commands, RG 338, NARA, in the WNRC. The Historical Section's command report collection is contained in 364 archives boxes.

Another series of reports of value to the researcher is the technical memorandums prepared by the Operations Research Office of G–3, General Headquarters, Far East Command, during the war. Most of these memorandums are narrowly focused on specific aspects of combat, manpower, or logistics. One, however, takes a broader view of general problems involved in supplying combat forces in Korea. Robert O. Shreve, Mary J. O'Brien, Alvin D. Coox, Owen F. Mattingly, and William H. Sutherland's "Combat Zone Logistics in Korea" (ORO-T-15 [FEC], Operations Research Office, General Headquarters, Far East Command, 1 December 1951) considers lines of communications with emphasis on transportation and frontline supply, maintenance support, and engineering support. The memorandum (actually a 200-page study) includes a logistical study of the Soyang River campaign from May to June 1951, concentrating on supply expenditure and its impact on transportation. Since the authors based their memorandum mostly on their own research in Korea and Japan from May to November 1951, their findings reflect the logistical situation as it was during that period. They do include, though, a discussion of the first two weeks of the war that employs war diaries and other record material. A copy of this memorandum is available in the library of the U.S. Army Center of Military History in Washington, D.C.; the other memorandums should be available in the records of the G-3 section of Headquarters, Far East Command, in RG 338. Huston employed these studies and incorporated many of their findings in "Korean Logistics."

Both Huston and the authors of the theater history, "Logistics in the Korean Operations," integrated into their work much of the information contained in a series of twenty manuscript monographs produced by the Historical Section, Headquarters, U.S. Army Forces, Far East-Eighth Army. For the most part, these monographs treat specific logistical facets or problems. Copies of some of the monographs may be found in the Records of the Office of the Chief of Military History in RG 319, NARA, in Washington, D.C. Presumably a full set exists in RG 338 at the WNRC, but confirmation of that assumption awaits further processing of the records by the National Archives.

In general, if the researcher requires or desires more detailed evidence than can be found in the command reports, he must seek it in the records of the Far East Command and subordinate commands in RG 338—not necessarily an easy quest. There is a draft inventory for the Far East Command records, but the description it provides is minimal. Arrangement of the records varies; all of the records of some staff sections are filed together, but there are also separate files, such as for general correspondence and for messages. Since the records of Headquarters, Far East Command, cover the entire command, not just Korea, the amount of material to be sifted through for the Korean War is just that much greater. Because of the lack of sufficient archival description, it is difficult even to locate the files of staff sections of some units. For tactical units, the problems of split accessions, arrangement, and coverage discussed earlier also apply.

A knowledgeable archivist at the Washington National Records Center estimates the quantities of records of various commands within the Far East Command for the period of the Korean War as follows: Headquarters, Far East Command, 1,500 linear feet; Eighth Army, 650 linear feet; Japan Logistical Command, 170 linear feet; 2d Logistical Command, 125 linear feet; 3d Logistical Command, unknown (location uncertain); Korean Communications Zone, 40 linear feet; Headquarters, U.S. Army Forces, Far East, 650 linear feet. This bulk, combined with the paucity of archival description, does not bode well for any attempt to construct a history of manpower and logistics in the theater principally from unit records. But with the voluminous command reports to rely on, the researcher hardly will lack for sources and probably will find that the unit records do not provide substantially more important information.

The thorough researcher will want to explore the personal papers of the three men who served as commander in chief, Far East Command, during the war. As cited earlier, the Ridgway papers are at the Military History Institute and the Clark papers at the Citadel. General of the Army Douglas MacArthur's papers reside in the MacArthur Memorial in Norfolk, Virginia.

There is almost no sustained treatment of theater manpower and logistics in the published memoirs of participants. Douglas MacArthur's *Reminiscences* (New York: McGraw-Hill, 1964) comments briefly on logistical difficulties during the drive north in October 1950. Ridgway's *The Korean War* and *Soldier* contain very little on manpower and logistics. Clark's *From the Danube to the Yalu* touches on rotation, which he finds disruptive of military efficiency, yet a necessity in a limited war in which only a tiny percentge of Americans were doing the fighting at any one time. In *Swords and Plowshares,* Taylor briefly discusses the ammunition controversy. He notes that artillery techniques contributed to the heavy usage that strained the supply system, but that supply was always sufficient to support essential needs. He repeats his remarks, mentioned above, on how entrenched the Eighth Army was in 1953 and his doubts about its ability to move to mobile warfare if the opportunity arose. After rotation began in 1951, he observes, the Eighth Army was never a completely trained fighting force; in 1953, the Korean Army Troops, U.S. Army, were the only real veterans in the Eighth Army.

A variety of views on logistics at a lower level may be found in John G. Westover's *Combat Support in Korea* (Washington, D.C.: Combat Forces Press, 1955). This collection of brief, edited interviews with officers and enlisted men who served in combat support units is divided into parts by the participants' branches, in addition to a potpourri of "short bits." Valuable for a feel of activities at the small-unit level, the book includes Westover's disclaimer that it is not history, but rather only a rendering of personal accounts.

CHAPTER 3

Toward a History of Mobilization and Logistics

The myriad of issues discussed in the foregoing bibliographic survey suggests the tremendous scope of any thorough history of Army mobilization and logistics in the Korean War. Taken together, the sources employed in the survey provide a solid base from which to pursue such a study. They supply at least partial answers to a great many important questions and raise other significant issues. The historian of mobilization and logistics can usefully frame a new study that builds on these questions, while adding inquiries and emphases of his own.

Kendall attacks what is perhaps the most basic question for the period between World War II and the Korean War: why did the United States find itself so unready to meet the crisis it faced in June 1950? His answers are persuasive: planners, preparing to fight a replay of the last war, did not come to grips with the possibility of waging a limited conventional war in the era of nuclear weapons; fiscal economy inhibited preparation; insufficient attention to the reserve components permitted them to deteriorate. Kendall has covered much ground that will not have to be trod again. His explanation of the Army's unreadiness to cope with deployment before expansion lays a good base for appraisal of events in wartime manpower mobilization.

In contrast, many questions about the state of readiness for industrial mobilization remain to be explored. The squabble between the National Security Resources Board and the Munitions Board needs to be examined in the primary sources, in terms of both ordinary bureaucratic turf battles and civil-military relations. This examination would seek effects of these battles and relations on industrial mobilization planning and on actual mobilization during the war. The content of the detailed annexes to the Industrial Mobilization Plan of 1947, and of the NSRB's revision of that plan, should be revealed to determine how closely mobilizers were able to adhere to prewar blueprints for their tasks — and how accurately the tasks were prefigured in the plans. In terms of readiness of plants to produce, what were the concrete results of the planning? A solid evaluation of the effects on industrial mobilization of deterioration in federally owned plants would also be instructive.

Prewar planning for the conduct of logistical operations in Korea, long thought to be a moot point because such planning had never existed, now must be investigated to resolve Colonel Curtis' claim of a 1948 strategic logistic study that envisioned war in Korea. This investigation would involve research in G-4 records in RG 319 and records of the Far East Command in RG 338.

The parlous condition of Far East Command units at the beginning of the war is well known and adequately treated in the literature. One facet of the response to the emergency that is worthy of further study is the efficacy of General MacArthur's expedient of throwing into the breach fillers with combat "potential." How well did these personnel from noncombat elements of the Far East Command perform? Another suitable object of study is the Career Guidance Program. Why was it allowed to impede the emergency response?

Then there is the question of supply readiness in the Far East Command. Should supply levels have been higher than they were, even though the North Korean invasion was unexpected? Normal supply procedures proved inadequate in the emergency, and it is fair to ask if that inadequacy should have been foreseen and corrected. Research might also discover whether the command's ability to meet a crisis was considered when the decision was made to place primary dependence for service support on local civilian employees—or whether there actually was such a decision. Perhaps the situation simply came about gradually as reliance on civilians gathered momentum.

A closer appraisal is required of how the readiness situation in the continental United States actually affected response. There is a need to separate a judgment of actual readiness for the Korean War from a judgment of readiness for war in Europe. While retaining the historical context in which decision makers had to operate—that is, the possibility of a larger war simultaneously with the one in Korea—the historian must not permit that context to dictate sole terms of evaluation. That the response to the Korean emergency seriously affected the residual mobilization base seems clear, but that response cannot be judged a failure simply on that ground alone. Keeping in mind the danger of weakness in the face of possible Soviet aggression elsewhere, the success of the reaction to the North Korean challenge must be judged by actual readiness in the face of that challenge.

Unbalanced and deteriorating U.S. equipment stocks present at least two questions. If tables of organization and equipment were changing in the years after World War II, did the changes provoke any notice that newly emphasized items were low in the stocks? Even if money was not available to bring the stocks into balance, was there at least official cognizance of the situation? And did cognizant officials speak out?

Though unbalanced, the World War II stocks provided an essential element of defense in 1950; similarly, the veterans of that war comprised a valuable pool of trained and experienced manpower. It would be very useful to arrive at some conclusions as to the importance of their contribution to training and combat. Case studies of training and combat units with high percentages of veterans, in comparison with other units, would be potentially rewarding. In a future mobilization, veterans of the Vietnam War would be too old to form a significant part of the mobilization base. It would be helpful to know, in rough terms, what effect their absence might have on mobilization and combat effectiveness.

Conceivably, light could be shed on other items of current interest to mobilization planners. Difficulties before and during the Korean War in keeping track of the status of individuals in unactivated reserve component units should be studied, if only for negative lessons. The dilemma of whether to recall reservists who held critical jobs in industry and government was largely a new one in the Korean War, but one that has persisted since. An examination of how decisions were made in such cases could have significant current value.

Politically sensitive decisions involving the National Guard in the late 1940s and early 1950s also are worthy of examination. Legal requirements for proportionate distribution of federal funds to states according to size of enrollment foiled Army plans to maintain selected guard units in a state of advanced readiness. How hard did the Army fight for selective advanced readiness? Was the battle obviously unwinnable? If so, why did the Army attempt the program? Finally—and perforce counterfactually—would selective readiness have produced debilitating morale problems in unselected units?

Political considerations demonstrably played a large role in the selection of National Guard units for federalization in 1950. But the ease of transportation for midwestern and western units to the West Coast also was a factor. Research might aim at discovering how large a potential problem transportation of units from the East actually represented.

The degree of autonomy that the National Guard enjoyed before federalization affected mobilization in other ways. According to

HERO's "Mobilization," more than half of the large number of National Guard discharges during the alert period in August 1950 were of guardsmen discovered to be under seventeen years of age. This fact raises the question of guard recruiting practices and procedures and the suspicion that underage recruits were knowingly accepted to raise strength figures. In addition, state adjutants general exercised their power to release men with dependents or in critical civilian occupations during the alert period. The criteria for these decisions beg to be explored. As a practical matter, however, a study of recruiting and release policies before federalization would require widespread research in records in the custody of the various states — to the extent that such records exist. A more modest undertaking would be to assay the effects of such policies on the readiness of guard units when mobilized.

Why did alerting, reporting, and processing policies and procedures present great difficulties? The answer is something of a puzzle, since the mobilization experience of World War II was relatively fresh and should have provided guidance. Research should aim to uncover the roots of policy in the late 1940s. Were there any attempts then to bring uniformity to the disparate policies of the services or, within the Army, to standardize the administrative procedures of the Regular Army, the National Guard, and the Organized Reserve Corps? Why was there so much confusion about induction delays and deferments? The problem of variations in procedure from one army area to another needs to be examined. Also, reasons should be sought for the lack of sufficient medical and trained administrative personnel in the units being inducted, and of medical personnel on the military district staffs. Were these simply shortages attributable to low budgets, or did they represent, at least in part, a lack of foresight? And the question of the National Guard's inability to convert to the Regular Army personnel record system, because of constraints on personnel levels and training time, requires investigation. Finally, the backsliding on reform measures brought on by the pressures of the Chinese intervention might serve as a valuable case study of the relationship between events on the battlefield and the procedures of mobilization. In general, the researcher with an eye to lessons usable in any future mobilization might well want to explore the mechanics of the Korean War mobilization in greater detail than anyone has heretofore.

Upon call-up, noncommissioned officers and officers from the reserve components required extra training to fit them for their cadre duties. Was it impossible to conduct this instruction, which disrupted unit training, before the units were alerted? Or would the expense have been too great and the personnel resources too small?

Competing needs during mobilization affected reserve component units adversely. The pressing need for personnel in the Far East Command dictated levies of mobilized units in training, with a predictable impact on morale at the training installations. The writers who deplore this effect suggest no viable alternative to meet the requirement for troops in the combat zone. One of the researcher's tasks might be to determine at what point, if any, the integrity of units in training should have outweighed the demands of the theater of operations. The positing of such a point would have to be accompanied by a plausible alternative strategy for protecting the Far East Command.

The problem of scarcity of equipment is more tangible and therefore should be easier for the historian to investigate. Of importance is the effect on mobilized units of equipment transfers to the Regular Army. These transfers were considerable in the first year of the war. Their impact should be studied in conjunction with the finding of HERO's "Mobilization" that lack of sufficient training equipment caused the Army to delay the mobilization of National Guard units in 1951. The HERO study cites a partial industrial mobilization as the cause of the postponement. Here is an opportunity for the historian, by means of one or more case studies, to make explicit connections between several aspects of mobilization, including readiness, training, procurement, and industrial mobilization. The research would span the records of units, training centers, Army Field Forces, Army staff agencies, and the emergency mobilization agencies.

Other case studies might seek to discover how newly constituted units were equipped. Probably, the answers could best be found in unit records, since the Army staff G-4 files on equipment are organized mainly by individual items. This aspect of mobilization has considerable potential relevance to the future.

Another aspect, of both historical and current interest, is the depletion of the mobilization base through a partial activation of the reserve components. Pre-Korean War plans did not allow for a situation in which a substantial part of the reserve forces were mobilized, leaving less than two-thirds of the total to cope with any other emergency that might arise. This is the other side of the coin of mobilization for the war. The historian in effect must balance the coin on edge and constantly rotate it, evaluating each side separately, and, at the same time, the two together. War with the Soviet Union was an unfulfilled but nonetheless real concern. A student of Korean War mobilization must be skillful in assessing both the actual mobilization and the feared one that never materialized. He must judge the former in absolute terms, apart from the latter, as a phenomenon unto itself. But he must also consider the real mobilization through the prism of the participants who viewed the specter of the other, unrealized one. Whether the coin should be kept spinning perpetually or allowed eventually to come to rest with one facet dominant is for him to decide.

In the course of making this decision, he might want to go further than HERO's "US Home Defense Forces Study" in examining the attempts of the states to cope with the need to replace mobilized National Guard forces. It is doubtful, however, that he would uncover much to challenge the conclusions of that study.

An area in which further investigation should prove fruitful is the Korean War draft. The connection between partial mobilization and the failure to abolish volunteering as a means of raising armies should be explored. In World War II the United States had to abandon volunteering because of its disruptive effects on draft call estimates and industry. Apparently, mobilization never reached the level during the Korean War at which volunteering threatened to upset either the wartime economy or the Selective Service System. The role of the armed services in retaining enlistment as a major source of manpower should be examined, and an evaluation made of Flynn's charge that military officials' aim was to use volunteering to "skim the cream" of the manpower supply. Also, it would be useful to determine to what extent the liberal deferment policy, which made draft quotas difficult to meet in the second half of 1951, was the result of a mobilization that was partial and therefore seemed less than urgent.

There are other draft-related issues. The staggered arrivals of draftees at training centers delayed training. Why could arrival schedules not be met? The demand for Regular Army personnel in Korea meant that draftees had to be trained by National Guard divisions. How well did this expedient work? On what bases can an evaluation be made?

Enormous replacement requirements in the Far East Command exerted strong pressures on units in training. An essential subject of investigation is the effects of cutting basic training time in order to help meet these demands. The historian may be able to find appraisals of basic trainees' readiness for combat in training records, or he may have to seek answers in the command reports of combat units.

Again the question of the impact of levies on the morale of reserve components in training arises. An evaluation of how badly levies hurt morale and delayed training schedules should be made. Refresher training for recalled reservists should be studied as to its content and adequacy and the degree to which it was affected by pressure from the Far East Command for speed. Commanders in Korea complained during the first nine months of the war about poor training and physical conditioning among replacements. The researcher, perhaps by case study, might tie the quality of replacements in Korea to the quality and duration of training in the United States.

In the theater, how did the Far East Command go about establishing its organization for replacement reception and training? What were the problems involved? And how did the command handle the need for reconstitution of badly depleted units such as the 7th Infantry Division? Finally, there are questions about the connection between battlefield success and replacement schedules. The optimistic outlook after the Inchon invasion caused a reduction in replacement schedules that proved costly when the outlook changed dramatically just a few months later. Should planners have been better prepared for this situation? If so, how?

Research is required to solve the discrepancy in the secondary sources over the role of replacements in the rotation system. The question is whether the first system required that a replacement be on hand before a soldier could be rotated. Once that point is settled, the historian would want to compare the merits of the first and second systems. If Stilwaugh is correct in her statement that the first system required that a replacement be present and that troops with sufficient time for rotation but without a replacement considered the system unfair, then was the second system, with its minimum rotation credits constantly fluctuating according to the availability of replacements, an improvement?

A detailed appraisal of the effects of the individual rotation policy and of the decision not to employ a general policy of unit rotation is desirable but has to be approached carefully. Case studies of units would seem the best way to proceed, but such studies would require information on soldiers' attitudes that might be incomplete or unavailable in unit records. Army staff G-3 and G-1 files and Far East Command reports would at least provide the bases on which decisions about rotation were made. Since the rotation program did not start until shortly before the beginning of the stalement in Korea, conclusions as to the program's success would have to be qualified to indicate that they did not reflect performance during a sustained war of movement.

There is little detail in the literature, outside of Huston's case study of the 2d Infantry Division, on the movement of troops to the theater. The emergency movement of the 2d Division in July 1950 deserves close study for lessons learned. Why were the normal preparations for overseas movement procedures so unwieldy and slow that they had to be modified or abandoned to meet the emergency of Korea? Did the failings stem from following too closely the experience of World War II, when such movements were planned long in advance? These are questions that Huston does not address. The historian also should study troop movements subsequent to that of the 2d Division to see whether procedures were further modified to meet events.

Of course, all of the soldiers who fought as part of the U.S. Army in Korea did not have to be transported; the Korean Army Troops, U.S. Army, were already there. The varying opinions, reviewed above, on the advantages and disadvantages of the KATUSA program demand a thorough investigation to arrive at well-documented, balanced conclusions.

Support of the men who fought involved a chain that led back to defense plants and the agencies that planned for and dealt with them in the United States. Of primary interest is the role of the National Security Resources Board during the critical early months of the war. Archival research is needed to examine the NSRB's efforts to supervise the gearing up of the economy for mobilization. Why did the agency have such apparently great difficulties? Particularly, why could it not get sufficient information on military requirements? Requirements had been a key source of dispute between the military and civilian mobilizers in the two world wars. The civilians had charged that the military either did not know its requirements or could not express them properly, and that in any case the claimed military needs were beyond the capacity of the nation to produce. This problem, although of lesser magnitude in a partial mobilization, is nevertheless at the center of civil-military relations in any industrial mobilization.

There is also a need for greater detail on the process and effects of moderating the pace of industrial mobilization while looking toward a gradual buildup for a possible future war with the Soviet Union. What was the impact, in both the United States and the Far East? To what extent were shortages of skilled workers and machine tools in defense industries tied to the purposeful restraint of mobilization?

That is, did the government not exert sufficient control over the economy to make these resources available for defense? In regard to the Far East, the researcher must ask to what degree industrial mobilization is relevant to the crucial first year of the war. With long lead times for major end items (even in the full mobilization of World War II, typically eighteen to twenty-four months), the nation did not achieve large-scale production until after the initial crisis had long passed. Here moderation of mobilization's pace could have had only an ancillary effect. From this perspective, the trials of the National Security Resources Board in 1950 are of interest mainly for their effect on production during the second half of the war. If the historian studies production of specific items, he should attempt to discover how requirements and programs for those items were altered by the change to static warfare in mid-1951.

Ammunition is one such item whose production might be studied. The ammunition shortage controversy by itself could easily provide the makings of a book-length study. But despite its complexity, the historian of Korean War mobilization and logistics should attempt to master the ammunition story because it contains implications for an assessment of various aspects of the war — prewar planning, industrial mobilization, and theater logistics.

Related to the moderated pace of industrial mobilization for a limited war was the continuing assumption by policy makers that the war would end within six months. Huston damns this assumption for its "crippling effect" on "effective logistic support." His assertion needs to be evaluated through two methods: first, an examination of the constraints that the assumption placed on procurement for support of the Far East Command and second — and more difficult — a judgment of the impact on operations. There appears to be a contradiction between Huston's claim here of ineffective logistic support and his charge, elsewhere, of oversupply. The discrepancy may be cleared up, at least partially, by a sharper focus on periodicity, with the oversupply coming later in the war.

Huston is more obviously on firm ground when he praises the rebuild program in Japan as an important supplier of the materiel needs of U.S. forces in Korea. Japan was a very convenient base for support activities. The historian would be well advised to measure closely the contribution of this island base to combat operations. His findings might provide a salutary antidote to any assumption that the U.S. Army necessarily could achieve in any trouble spot what it did in Korea.

Another assumption, one implicit in the literature on logistics during the Korean War, is that the Army's logistical system in the United States functioned so well as not to require a critique. Huston's comment on the seeming ponderousness of the system should serve as an alert to the need for archival research.

Logistical organization in the theater presents several questions for the historian. Doctrine called for the establishment of TOE logistical commands. The commands that the Army set up, although table of distribution and allowances units, were based on tables of organization and equipment, and they suffered many problems. Was the doctrine at fault for tying commanders to rigid TOEs? The theater history absolves the doctrine of fault but still maintains that the tables of organization and equipment employed were too inflexible for the variety of missions that the commands had to perform. There is an inconsistency here that must be addressed.

Was the setup of the Korean Communications Zone and the Korean Base Section, with their overlapping functions, the most efficient organization possible under the circumstances? Why did it take so long for even this organization, with its imperfections, to evolve? The establishment of Headquarters, U.S. Army Forces, Far East, which absorbed the Japan Logistical Command, complicated the relationship between the headquarters in Japan and the Korean Communications Zone in Korea. Partial regularization of this anomaly did not come until 1953. Was the lateness of this attempt to bring theater logistical organization more in line with doctrine the result of contradictory doctrinal tendencies toward centralized control and command flexibility?

One of the most intriguing questions involving organization is the cause of the inadequate logistical liaison between the Eighth Army and the X Corps. This poor coordination helped delay the advance to the Yalu and complicated the movement of the X Corps to the east coast of Korea in the fall of 1950. There should have been ample precedent from both world wars to enable the commanders involved to meet the challenge of coordination with less difficulty. Why they did not is for the historian to discover.

In establishing requirements doctrine before the Korean War, logisticians were explicit in their use of World War II precedents. As suggested previously, a cold war orientation toward Europe may explain the employment of European Theater of Operations experience in setting consumption levels and replacement factors. But the historian might also explore the possibility that the World War II service of those writing and approving the doctrine was primarily in Europe.

Further, the researcher would perform a service by isolating those elements affecting requirements in the Korean situation that were unusual or that appear to be unique. This information would be of value to current and future requirements planners.

Conditions largely apart from the physical environment in Korea are also said to have affected requirements. The theater logistical history suggests that the standard of living for U.S. troops in Korea was maintained at a level incompatible with the need to husband resources for possible combat elsewhere. Is this claim supportable in view of the Truman administration's general approach to the Korean War, in which Europe always loomed so large? Study is also needed of alleged oversupply and supply indiscipline in Korea. Case studies would be applicable here, if the data is available.

Huston warns that "it is almost impossible to arrive at figures which will give a completely accurate picture" of the extent of the supply effort in Korea. He explains that

in part this is because little [*sic*] or no records were kept on many items in the days of hectic shipments during the early weeks of the conflict. More important is the fact that it practically is impossible to eliminate duplication in figures giving tonnage of supplies shipped to Korea. Figures are available on total shipments from the continental United States to Japan and Korea, and some figures can be found on shipments from Japan to Korea; but there is no way of eliminating all the duplication which would result from adding those figures.[1]

In elaboration, Huston states that "accurate figures on actual quantities of individual clothing and equipment items shipped to Korea are almost impossible to obtain. Shipments had to include supplies for building up reserve stocks as well as for immediate use; they included initial issues of certain items of equipment to some units and not to others; figures on bulk shipments give no indication of the quantities which accompanied units and replacements moving to Korea."[2] The theater history itself observes that "especially during the early period of hostilities, the accurate recording of receipts and issues was not accomplished at the base depots in Korea. In addition, repairable equipment, salvage, and turn-ins of excess or unauthorized equipment were included in the figures of overall receipts. Net

---

[1]Huston, "Korean Logistics," ch. VI, p. 1.
[2]Ibid., ch. X, pp. 24–25.

receipts in Korea of supplies and equipment from outside sources were therefore difficult to determine."[3]

Although these statements emphasize the war's early phase, they clearly refer in general to the entire span of the conflict. Add to their caveats the probable destruction or disappearance of some supply records over the past three decades (such archival losses are common and seem inevitable), and the difficulty of accurately appraising supply quantity and discipline becomes apparent.

Much work remains to be done in the study of the distribution system. Huston relates the development of the PINK emergency shipment of equipment for an entire division and says that such shipments became standard operating procedure. The researcher might follow up to see how PINK was employed, how often, and with what success after the initial usage.

Further research is needed on the experience that led up to the modification of the system of automatic supply. This modification did not come until the summer of 1951. Did the fluid tactical situation in the war's first year preclude earlier change?

Why did logisticians never reach their goal of having one-half of all shipments from the United States go directly to Korea? The explanation by U.S. Army Forces, Far East, that the failure resulted from a decrease in the intensity of the war, combined with a backlog of lumber in Japan, should be examined. The influence of inadequate port facilities in Korea should be considered.

According to the secondary sources, most supplies from the United States went to Korea by ship because of the expense of air shipment. Explicit connections might be sought between budget constraints and the restriction of air transport. Also, some informed speculation might be in order as to whether reliance on slower water shipment affected the tactical situation in Korea significantly.

Why were supply accountability procedures unable to keep track efficiently of items stocked in depots in Japan? Granting the great variety and volume of items, did World War II not provide sufficient experience in the handling of such problems? To what degree were the number and training of supply personnel a factor?

Problems connected with ports in Korea were numerous and of a type that is of continuing interest to logisticians. Limited port facilities in Korea made LSTs valuable, and Huston mentions a possible shortage of them in the Far East Command. If there was a short-

---

[3]"Logistics in the Korean Operations," vol. II, frame 43.

age, it raises the question of what had happened to the great quantity of LSTs used for amphibious operations in World War II. The question is especially interesting in view of the fact that planners before the Korean War expected that the next conflict would be similar to World War II.

There is a need to study the Army's relations with Korean and Japanese stevedores. How did the Army go about ameliorating problems of language, theft, breakage, and labor disputes in the Korean ports? How heavy a reliance did the Army actually place on mobile Japanese labor gangs berthed on barracks ships? And what were the Army's relations with these Japanese laborers?

Research is also required on the actual discharge capacities of Korean ports at various times during the war. The influence of personnel and transportation difficulties on these capacities should be examined closely. It is clear that the location of depots at the ports contributed to congestion because of inadequate transportation to move materiel to the interior. But it is not clear if Huston's criticism of the depots' location is balanced. The researcher might ask where the depots might have been established instead. Might the location of depots outside the ports have taxed transportation facilities even more, by requiring more short hauls and more unloadings?

Huston's question about an alternative to the rail system in Korea is a very important one. He presents evidence that there were insufficient numbers of trucks to take up the supply burden if the rail system, which operated constantly at full capacity, failed. The historian should seek to ascertain the validity of this claim.

Another very significant question involves the failure to establish intermediate depots. While it seems plain that they would have been useful, it is not certain that the logistical personnel needed to man them were available. Besides investigating the personnel aspect, the historian might ask how much emphasis commanders at various levels put on the need for such depots. He would also do well to examine expedients, such as informal truck convoys, that the divisions employed to get supplies from Pusan to the troops. These expedients seem to have developed in response to the lack of intermediate depots—a lack that strained rail lines.

Much more detailed information is needed on the system of supply points, back-up points, and regulating points, including their distance from each other and their operating procedures. Were their locations and procedures adequate for their functions? Huston believes that various difficulties justified the location of supply points farther to the rear than the divisions being supplied would have liked. His conclusion should be tested.

An examination of Korean hand carriers could be a study in itself. An extended study would be worthwhile because the carriers formed the essential last link in the supply chain. It would be useful to determine whether the militarization of hand carriers significantly increased their efficiency. And it would be interesting to know how much more than hand carriers the importation of pack animals would have cost, and what problems the use of animals might have entailed.

The issue of U.S. logistical support for United Nations and Republic of Korea forces is not treated sufficiently in the literature. Although United Nations forces other than those of the United States and the Republic of Korea never totaled more than 10 percent of the combined allied troop strength, their partial support presented problems for the Army's distribution system. Huston and the theater history give some attention to the difficulties of supplying rations to suit various national tastes and to the intricacies of reimbursement, but do not explain exactly what impact these problems had on the Army's supply system. Similarly, there is information in these two sources on the costs of providing 90 percent of the ROK Army's support and on the peculiarities of Korean logistical practices, but little on how the extra burden affected overall distribution. Current U.S. plans call for U.S. responsibility for the support of all allied forces in any operations outside Europe. More detailed knowledge of such support in the Korean War, therefore, should be of considerable value to the U.S. Army.

Finally, the historian of Korean War logistics should be careful to draw explicit connections between logistical activities and field operations. Logistics, after all, derives its raison d'etre from its relation to operations. For logisticians and tacticians alike, much of the importance of the experience in Korea lies in the fluidity of the tactical situation in the war's first year. The events of that year provide an opportunity to study how the Army's logistical system coped with the quite opposite problems of rapid advance and retreat within a relatively short period of time.

After a review of the issues and the sources, it is patent that the history of U.S. Army mobilization and logistics in the Korean War is a very large area for study. The number of questions to be posed is legion and the volume of record material vast. But it seems clear that the exploration of this history can contribute not only to our understanding of the Korean War experience, but also to the solution of current problems in planning for mobilization and logistics.

Author Index

Title Index

GPO U.S. GOVERNMENT PRINTING OFFICE: 2011 369-843